Just Read the Story in the Leaves

Tea leaf reading is a skill anyone can master. Simply pour yourself a cup of tea, pull up a chair, and open *Tea Leaf Reading*. With a bit of practice and guidance from the author, you'll quickly learn how to interpret the arrangement of the leaves and "read the story" written in them for your friends, family, and yourself.

Reading tea leaves has been done for as long as people have been drinking tea. William Hewitt's mother taught him this venerable art when he was a child, and he has practiced this form of divination all his life. Here he reveals his expert insights, secrets, and tips for reading the leaves like a professional. These techniques will do more than help you accurately predict the future—they'll also develop your innate psychic ability and give you a clearer understanding of life's mysteries.

About the Author

William W. Hewitt was born on July 4, 1929, in Toledo, Ohio to a loving, gifted woman who was psychic and an expert at reading tea leaves. Her son learned these skills, becoming an expert at interpretation. Now a successful author, he has developed his own innate psychic ability.

Now retired, Mr. Hewitt has more than 20 years experience as a professional hypnotherapist. As a published author, he has written 12 books (nine of which are still in print) and numerous magazine articles on hypnosis, psychic development, astrology, self help. Mr. Hewitt has also published a number of children's stories. In retirement he still continues to write and gives lectures on hypnosis, psychic development, and self help.

To Write to the Author

If you wish to contact the author or would like more information about this book, please write to the author in care of Llewellyn Worldwide and we will forward your request. Both the author and the publisher appreciate hearing from you and learning of your enjoyment of this book and how it has helped you. Llewellyn Worldwide cannot guarantee that every letter written to the author can be answered, but all will be forwarded. Please write to:

William W. Hewitt
C/o Llewellyn Worldwide
P.O. Box 64383, Dept. K391-3
St. Paul, MN 55164-0383

Please enclose a self-addressed, stamped envelope for reply, or $1.00 to cover costs. If outside U.S.A., enclose international postal reply coupon.

Tea Leaf Reading

William W. Hewitt

1998
Llewellyn Publications
St. Paul, Minnesota, U.S.A.

SECOND EDITION
First printing, 1998

First edition, two printings, 1989

Cover design by Lisa Novak
Cover photograph by Leo Tushaus
Symbol illustrations by Norman B. Stanley and Lisa Novak
Second edition editing and design by Christine Snow

Library of Congress Cataloging-in-Publication Data
Hewitt, William W., 1929–
    Tea leaf reading / William W. Hewitt. -- 2nd ed.
      p. cm.
    Includes index.
    ISBN 1-56718-391-3 (alk. paper)
    1. Fortune-telling by tea leaves.   I. Title.
BF1881.H49 1998
133.3'244--dc21   98-23761
                                   CIP

Llewellyn Publications
A Division of Llewellyn Worldwide, Ltd.
P.O. Box 64383, Dept. K391-3
St. Paul, MN 55164-0383

Printed in the U.S.A.

Other Books by William Hewitt

Hypnosis for Beginners (1997)

Self-Hypnosis for a Better Life (1997)

Psychic Development for Beginners (1996)

The Truth About Mind Power (1994)

The Truth About the Power in Your Birth Chart (1994)

Bridges to Success & Fulfillment (1993)

The Truth About Hypnosis (1993)

Astrology for Beginners (1991)

Audio Tapes

Become Smoke Free Through Self-Hypnosis

The Psychic Workout Through Self-Hypnosis

Relaxation and Stress Management Through Self-Hypnosis

Your Perfect Weight Through Self-Hypnosis

*This book is dedicated to
my wife, Dee, whose love and support
are vitally important to me …
and to the memory of my mother,
Dorothy Agnes Hewitt.*

Contents

Preface to the Second Edition

Growing up as a child in the 1930s I was vaguely aware that my mother had frequent visitors with whom she had tea and the visitors would ask questions and my mother would look into a tea cup thoughtfully and answer the questions. At that time it made no special impression on my youthful mind which was more interested in going out to play.

Then in 1941, the United States was drawn into World War II, and the frequency of the "tea" visits to our house grew to everyday events. The women visitors were asking questions about their husbands, sons and loved ones who were suddenly taken away to serve in the armed forces. They wanted to know if they would be safe. How would they manage to survive and take care of things at home with their men gone? And a myriad of other very serious questions.

When the United States entered the war, I was twelve years old and I started to take a more mature view of what was happening in the world. I started listening to what my mother was telling these tea visitors. How did my mother come up with the information she gave the visitors? And even more importantly, what was going on when the visitors returned to tell my mother that she had been 100 percent accurate with her predictions?

So I asked my mother. She told me that she read the information in the tea leaf patterns in the visitors' tea cups, and asked me if I would like to learn how to do it.

I said, "Yes." And thus began my introduction into the psychic world of tea leaf reading and ultimately into many other aspects of the psychic world.

For years tea leaf reading was just a game to me and I gave no serious thought as to why it worked. It worked, and that was all I cared about. As an adult with a family, I read the leaves for my wife and children. It was just a fascinating pastime.

Many years later, driven by some spontaneous psychic experiences, I was drawn into a lengthy investigation of psychic matters and began writing books about my experiences and what I had learned.

My first two books for Llewellyn Publications were selling well. Llewellyn's Acquisitions Manager, Nancy Mostad, phoned to ask me what I was going to write next for them. I answered, "Nancy, everything I know in the whole world is in the two books you have already published."

Nancy didn't accept that and she carefully prodded me to talk about my life. While talking, I mentioned I knew how to read tea leaves. She quickly interrupted me with "That's it! Write us a book about tea leaf reading." I said I would think about it but didn't know if I could remember everything.

Being a hypnotist, I used self-hypnosis to recall all my mother had taught me. I wrote this book, *Tea Leaf Reading*, as a tribute to my mother who was a natural born psychic who had learned from her mother, who had learned from her mother before her and so on, back through a long lineage of tea leaf readers.

Like my mother and me, you too can learn to read tea leaves and open up your own avenues into your psychic development.

This second edition of *Tea Leaf Reading* pleases me greatly. It gives a new, modern look to an old divination skill. More symbol interpretations have been added to the extensive glossary along with a number of new illustrations to aid you in learning and practicing tea leaf reading more easily.

I hope you enjoy the book and I would like to hear from you. If you send a stamped, addressed return envelope I will be delighted to answer your letter.

—William W. Hewitt
May, 1998

Introduction

The future already exists in the non-physical world, even though it hasn't yet occurred in the physical world. This phenomenon has intrigued people since the dawn of time. Nothing piques the imagination more than the possibility that one might be able to take a peek into the future.

Can that really be done? Is it really possible to see into the future? Yes. It can be done! Prophecy has always existed. There have always been people who could accurately predict the future. Joseph foresaw the future through his dreams and advised the Pharaoh. The French astrologer Nostradamus made predictions that spanned several centuries. Edgar Cayce, the American psychic, made thousands of accurate divinations about the future. Ancient seers advised the powerful men and women who ruled nations such as Julius Caesar, who was warned about the Ides of March but ignored the warning and was murdered.

There have been thousands of men and women throughout history who learned how to peek into the future. Some used the stars. Some, dreams. Some used cards. Some, crystal balls. Others just seemed to know things. Many used various other means to focus their awareness on things "yet to come."

My mother was one of these people. She read tea leaves. I learned from her, and now I pass my knowledge on to you because tea leaf reading is a skill nearly everyone can master quickly and inexpensively.

Tea leaf reading is a great social catalyst. Friends and family can have hours of enjoyment and conversation while reading each other's cups. Of course, you can read your own cup for your own edification.

It is also a beneficial pastime because it is possible to answer questions accurately and peek into the future. Forewarned is half armed. The more knowledge you have, the better you are able to deal with a situation.

This book provides the following:

Tells you the philosophy of tea leaf reading so you will understand why it works.

Tells you how to prepare the tea cup for reading.

Tells you how to analyze and read all the tea leaf symbols.

Tells you how to interpret the symbols you see in the cup.

Provides an extensive glossary of symbols with their meanings so you can begin to interpret the tea leaves immediately.

Gives you a bonus. The Appendix contains information about quartz crystals that can aid you in reading tea leaves, or it may help you in some other interesting pursuits.

Provides an index to quickly refer you to the symbols in the glossary. The index cross-references many symbols so that you are likely to find what you need.

Philosophy of Tea Leaf Reading

Each person radiates a powerful energy field called an aura. This is a fact. Auras can be photographed with Kirilian photography.

A person's aura extends about three feet in every direction from the person. The aura permeates everything with which it comes in contact.

The energy, intelligence, frequencies, emotions, and vibrations of each person's aura are unique to that person. No two are alike.

Now consider this. Every cell in a person's body contains 100 percent of all the information about that person—past, present, and future. Not only that, but every cell also contains a hologram of the universe; that is, all knowledge is resident within each one of us, and it is ours to retrieve if we know how.

Tea leaves seem to be one substance that is easily influenced by exposure to a person's aura, so it follows logically that if you expose tea leaves to a person's aura, the leaves can cluster to symbolically record information from that exposure.

It is further logical that if one knows how to read and interpret the exposed tea leaf clusters, information can be obtained about the person whose aura influenced the tea leaves. Simply stated: a person prepares a cup of tea. The tea leaves record information about that person. The leaves can then be read to reveal the recorded information.

Easy. And it works.

I don't purport that tea leaf reading is the most powerful method for answering questions, looking into the future, revealing the past, or analyzing the present. It isn't. I teach more powerful methods in my books *Hypnosis for Beginners (Llewellyn, 1997)* and *Psychic Development for Beginners (Llewellyn, 1996)*.

However, the more powerful methods require heavy duty commitment and disciplined training. Of course, these produce profound, heavy duty results.

Tea leaf reading is different. It is lighthearted, fun, and requires very little except an open mind and a spirit of adventure. The results are accurate and startling. You may not learn everything there is to know by reading tea leaves, but you will learn enough to make it well worth your while.

There are three uses of tea leaf readings:

To prophesy the present time. This is for the period from the time the reading is given through the following twelve months. This is the most common use of tea leaf reading, and this book is slanted principally toward "present time" readings. Only one tea cup is needed to do a twelve-month prophecy.

To answer a specific question. This can be very useful. The problem is that only one question can be answered with each tea cup. Thus, it becomes quite time consuming if you want to answer a series of questions. This will be discussed later.

To examine the past. This is not widely practiced because it isn't especially useful, and the cup does not usually give any time references. This will also be mentioned, superficially, later.

Preparing the Tea Cup

The person for whom the reading is to be done should prepare his or her own cup of tea whenever possible. Later I will describe what to do if the person is not able to prepare their own cup due to physical problems or because they are not physically present.

For now, *assume that you are going to prepare the cup of tea to read for yourself.*

Get a clean tea cup and saucer. Cups that aren't clean may have residue on the sides and bottom that could prevent the leaves from orienting themselves naturally, thus not giving an accurate reading.

Do not use a mug. Mugs have vertical sides and generally have a smaller opening than a tea cup, making it nearly impossible to properly disperse the leaves and to read the leaves accurately.

Use loose tea leaves. If you only have tea bags, tear the bag open and dump the contents into the cup. I recommend you purchase some loose tea instead of using tea bags. This is because tea bags have more finely ground tea which has a tendency to "clump" rather than form patterns, thus providing less information for you to work with.

If you intend to drink the tea before reading the leaves, do not use sweetener or milk of any kind. This is because sweeteners and milk make the leaves sticky. Sticky leaves will not orient themselves naturally either, thus giving inaccurate information.

Follow these steps:

1. Put the loose tea into the cup, approximately one-half teaspoonful.

2. Pour very hot water on the leaves, enough to cover them. Hot water makes the leaves more supple than cold water, thus enhancing their ability to form patterns. *Note:* If you want to drink the tea before reading the leaves, fill up the cup with hot water and brew the tea to your liking. Then drink the tea, making sure to leave enough water to cover the leaves.

3. Now you want to impregnate the tea leaves with your energy. If you make a cup of tea and drink it, you will make sufficient contact to energize the tea leaves.

If you just prepared a small solution of tea and water, you can energize it like this: place the palm of one hand over the top of the cup and leave it there for one to two minutes.

4. Place a napkin or paper towel on a saucer and set it aside. This will absorb excess water in a few moments.

5. Now comes the important step of dispersing the leaves around the inside of the cup while getting rid of the water ("sloshing").

Proceed as follows: Hold the cup's handle and use wrist motion to gently and slowly slosh the water around the entire inside of the cup. As you rotate and slosh the mixture, allow the cup to tip sufficiently for small amounts of water to spill over the top and drip into a sink or bowl. Continue until the water is gone and the tea leaves are dispersed around the inside of the cup.

It may take practice for you to develop the technique of dispersing the leaves while getting rid of the water and not losing all of the leaves.

A couple notes: you will probably lose a few tea leaves during the "sloshing" process. This is to be expected so don't be concerned about it. During the sloshing, if you go too slowly, the leaves will tend to bunch in one large clump. If you go too fast, the leaves won't stick to the sides of the cup. With a little practice, you will master the technique. In any case, use the cup however it turns out because it will still contain valid information.

6. Turn the cup upside down and place it on the napkin/paper towel on the saucer. This will absorb the remaining few drops.

7. Set the cup, still upside down in the saucer, in front of you.

8. Rotate the cup three revolutions in a clockwise direction. This accomplishes two things: it dislodges any remaining drops of water, and it gives your aura an additional chance to impregnate the leaves.

9. Pick the cup up by the handle and turn it right side up. The cup may now be read.

Preparing the Cup for Someone Else

Earlier I mentioned that there may be times when the person may be unable to prepare their own cup. Here is what to do in those situations.

When the Person Is Physically Present

In these cases the person is probably physically disabled or bedridden but is present for the reading. Prepare the cup just as the though you were going to prepare it for yourself except for the energizing part. Before you begin the sloshing process, place the cup in front of the person, well within the person's aura, and leave it there for five minutes. Make sure that you are at least six feet away from the cup for this five-minute period. Then proceed with the reading as described earlier.

When the Person Is Not Physically Present

There may be times when you will be asked to do a reading for someone who is somewhere else, perhaps in another town or even in another country. This can be done, but it calls for special effort on the part of the one doing the reading. You must act as a channel for the energy of the other person.

Prepare the cup just as you would if you were reading for yourself. When it comes time to energize the leaves, you must concentrate your thoughts on the name and location of the person for whom you are doing the reading.

Here is a suggestion: write the name, age, sex, and address of the person on a piece of paper. Hold that piece of paper while you place the palm of your hand over the tea cup. Close your eyes and mentally say, "I desire to energize these tea leaves with the energy of (name of person) in order to obtain an accurate reading for (name of person)."

Then open your eyes and proceed to read the leaves. This process will work because every cell in your body contains a hologram of the universe which, of course, includes information of the person for whom you are reading. Some people learn to do this more quickly and effectively than others.

Just keep at it and you will succeed.

Preparing the Cup to Answer a Question

Have the question written on a piece of paper. The person who energizes the tea leaves should hold the paper and concentrate on the question while doing the energizing. If possible, the question should be written so the answer is more than just a simple yes or no because you will get more information. For example, don't ask, "Will I ever find a better job?" Instead ask, "What are my future employment possibilities?" The second question opens up many more possibilities for providing details, and it still answers the question of yes or no.

Analyzing the Tea Cup

For present time readings, the cup will display twelve months of information. Figure 3-1 on page 12 is a drawing of the cup as you look down into it. Study the time zones of the cup that are labeled.

You always read the cup in a clockwise direction starting at the left edge of the handle. Symbols near the left edge of the handle relate to events or situations that are going to occur within a day to a couple weeks. Those that appear one-quarter of the way around will occur in about three months, and so forth as shown in the drawing, until you reach one

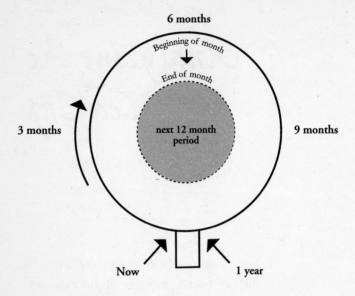

FIGURE 3-1: Time zones of the tea cup

year at the right edge of the handle. Symbols near the rim of the cup relate to the beginning of a monthly period. The further down the side of the cup the symbol appears, the further into the monthly period. For example: if a bird in flight appeared one-fourth of the way around the cup (approximately three months from now) and about halfway down the side of the cup (halfway through the third month), you could say, "You will be receiving some good news approximately three and a half months from now."

The word "now" is used here to mean the time that the reading is being given, so if the reading was on June 17, you could say (for the example just given), "You will be receiving good news around the end of September or early October."

For time periods between the quarter marks shown on the drawing you will have to give your best estimate. For example, halfway between three months and six months is approximately four and a half months, and so on.

Notice in the drawing that the bottom of the cup (shown in the small dotted circle) contains information that is valid throughout the next twelve-month period. *This pertains only to those symbols that are on the flat bottom,* not to symbols near the bottom. If a symbol is partly on the side of the cup and partly on the bottom, interpret it as though it were only on the side which would indicate the last one or two days of that monthly period and then continuing throughout the remainder of the twelve-month period. For example, suppose a reading was given on May 1. A four-leaf clover appears three-fourths of the way around the cup, partly on the side of the cup and partly on the bottom. You could then say, "You will have a period of great good fortune beginning the end of next February and extending to next May first."

When you start to read the cup, take a few minutes to study it thoroughly. Look at it from many angles, even with the cup upside down. Look for groups of symbols (couples). Look for those symbols that stand alone and are not a part of any group. Take care as you turn the cup so you don't dislodge the tea leaves. Do not touch or rearrange the leaves. When you have a good idea of what symbols are in the cup, you may proceed to interpret them as described in Chapter 4, "Interpreting Tea Leaf Symbols."

For a Past Time Reading

Past time readings can sometimes be helpful in understanding why things are the way they are at the present time. Also, past time readings can sometimes help a person release the past so they can begin to live in and enjoy the present.

The time segments of the cup have no validity. You only can give a relative time reading. Symbols nearer the cup handle as you read clockwise occurred closer to the present time than those that appear farther from the handle. However, there is no way of knowing (other than an intuitive guess) how long ago something occurred.

You probably won't have many requests for past lifetime readings. The present and near future are what most people want to know about, and that is the thrust of this book.

To Answer a Specific Question

If you are doing the reading to answer a specific question, the time segments of the cup have no validity. Here you just study the symbols and groups of symbols in relation to the specific question. Then you give the answer. This will be discussed in more detail in the next chapter.

~ 4 ~

Interpreting Tea Leaf Symbols

This is the fun part—interpreting the tea leaf symbols to make an accurate, informative forecast.

All you need to do to interpret a cup is to prepare and analyze the cup as previously discussed and then look up each symbol in the Symbol Glossary (Chapter 5), or use the index for easier location. Then put together a scenario that tells the story. I'll give several example interpretations shortly.

The comprehensive glossary of symbols and their meanings are those that I have encountered, and the meanings I have found to be accurate over years of study and practice. Throughout the glossary, I explain how to interpret different shades of meaning and varying situations.

I also recommend that you keep a written record of your readings, at least when you first start reading tea leaves, so you can monitor the accuracy and completeness of your forecasts. This is how you learn and perfect your technique.

For a Present Time Reading

The tea cup is prepared for the person for whom the reading is being done. In this book I'll refer to that person as "you." If some of the information shown in the cup pertains to someone other than you, the cup will indicate that by using a symbol for someone else such as a figure of a person, a horse, a dog, etc.

If two symbols in the tea cup are less than one-quarter inch apart, they are close enough to influence each other. In this book I refer to symbols that influence each other as being "coupled" (grouped). Coupled simply means that you must blend the interpretation of both symbols together in order to obtain the most accurate meaning.

For example, suppose a bee and a desk are less than a quarter-inch apart, near the cup rim, just to the left of the cup handle. Look up *Bee* in the glossary: it says gossip. Look up *Desk*: it refers to your work. The meaning of this bee/desk symbol coupling indicates that there is gossip about you at your work place that is happening now or will take place within the next few days.

The glossary tells you in detail how to interpret each symbol. It gives you the symbolic meaning with various shades of interpretation as well as key words for quick reference, the polarity of each symbol, and when to interpret it literally.

The polarity of a symbol will either be positive, negative, or neutral. Frequently you will see an entry in the glossary that says something like, "If this symbol is coupled with a negative symbol, then interpret it as...." Or, "If this symbol is coupled with a positive symbol then interpret it as...." For example, read the interpretation for *Hat* in the glossary. Many other symbols will have similar statements.

In these cases of polarity, you just look up the symbols that are coupled with each other to see what their polarities are. Then you have your interpretation.

Some symbols are always interpreted literally; that is, they always mean exactly what they appear to be. These are identified in the glossary for those few cases.

Most symbols are usually symbolic. But some may, under certain conditions, also be interpreted literally. In these cases the glossary will have a statement like this: "*Literal meaning:* If a (symbol) is coupled with a numeral or an alphabetic letter, interpret the symbol literally as being a (symbol)." For example, look up *Ship* (you will find it under the *Boat* listing) in the glossary. If any number (1, 2, 3, etc.) or any alphabetic letter (a, b, c, etc.) is within a quarter-inch (coupled) of the ship symbol in the cup, then interpret the symbol as meaning "ship." The numerals and alphabetic letters are the significators for identifying when to interpret a symbol literally. Each of these cases is described in the glossary.

Chances are that the glossary will contain sufficient information to enable you to do a complete and accurate interpretation. However, if you see a symbol that is not in the glossary, look to see if there is something similar to help guide you. For example, you see a sparrow in a cup. The glossary doesn't have *Sparrow* but it does have *Bird.*

Occasionally, you will see a symbol that doesn't relate closely to anything in the glossary. In this case, you must make your best intuitive guess as to the meaning in relation to the rest of the cup. This is why keeping written records is helpful. You can verify the accuracy of your intuitive guess and thus expand your knowledge. For example, I have never seen a roulette wheel symbol in a cup, but if I did I would intuitively know it meant "risk."

Example Interpretation #1

Assumption: The reading is done on January 1.

The symbols in the cup: There is a bird perched in a tree halfway around the cup near the bottom. This makes the bird and the tree "coupled." (See Figure 4-1.)

Analyze the cup: First look up *Bird (perched),* and *Tree* in the glossary. The generic perched bird means that you are waiting to hear from someone. The tree pertains to your family. The position in the cup indicates near the end of the sixth month from now.

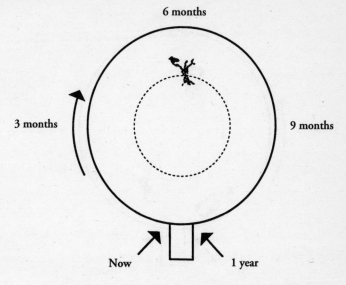

FIGURE 4-1: **Cup for Example Interpretation #1**

Interpretation: About the end of July you will be waiting, probably anxiously, to hear from some member of your family. You will be expecting to hear and it will be important to you. Nothing you see in the tea cup is ever unimportant.

Example Interpretation #2

Assumption: The reading is given on January 1.

The symbols in the cup: There is a bottle near the cup rim just to the left of the cup handle. There is a light bulb about halfway between the three-month and six-month position at the bottom. There is a monkey just to the right of the handle near the bottom

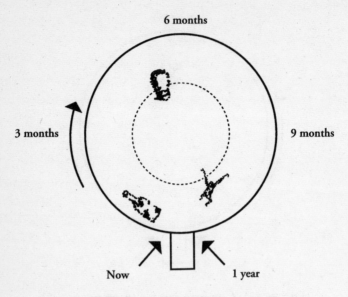

FIGURE 4-2: Cup for Example Interpretation #2

but not on the bottom. No symbols are coupled
with any of these. (See Figure 4-2.)

Analyze the cup: Look up *Bottle, Light Bulb,* and
Monkey in the glossary. The bottle means you will be
faced with a temptation, and its position indicates
between now and the next week or two. The light
bulb means you will burn up energy, and its position
indicates from about mid-May and continuing at
least through the end of the year. The monkey means
you will behave foolishly, and its position indicates
about mid to end of December.

Interpretation: Sometime between now and the next week or two you will be tempted to do something that is unwise for you to do. If you give in to the temptation, it will return to haunt you and cause you grief sometime later in your life. If you choose to not give in to the temptation, you will emerge a stronger and better person for it. It is your choice to be strong or weak. Your choice will affect the rest of your life.

From about mid-May through the rest of the year you will have an abundance of energy. You will burn up this energy sometimes on achievement and worthwhile activities. Other times you will burn your energies up on wasteful activities.

Near the end of the year you will find yourself behaving quite foolishly. Even though there are no detrimental indications in your cup, you should try to hold your foolish behavior down because such behavior can damage your reputation in the eyes of others and in your own eyes also.

Example Interpretation #3

Assumption: The reading is given on January 1.

Symbols in the cup: A three-leaf clover, all by itself, on the bottom of the cup. There is a box within a quarter-inch of a dog; a quarter-inch away on the other side of the dog is the numeral "1." These are three-fourths of the way around the cup. (See Figure 4-3 on page 22.)

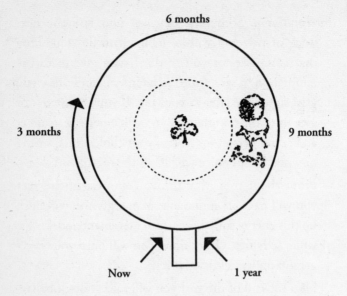

FIGURE 4-3: Cup for Example Interpretation #3

Analyze the cup: Look up *Clover, Box, Dog,* and *Numeral.* Clover indicates good fortune, and its position at the bottom of the cup means the entire year is affected. A box means you will receive a gift. A dog is coupled to a numeral, so it is interpreted literally as being a dog. These all appear about nine months from now.

Interpretation: You will have a good year that is filled with good fortune in general. In addition, you will receive a dog as a gift about September (nine months from the time the reading is given in January).

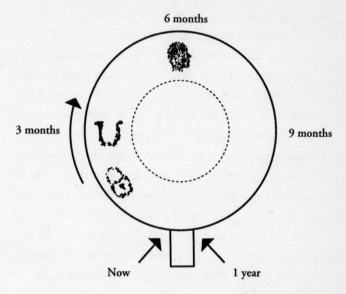

FIGURE 4-4: **Cup for Example Interpretation #4**

Example Interpretation #4

Assumption: The reading is given on January 1.

Symbols in the cup: There is a padlock halfway between the cup handle and the three-month position near the rim. A horseshoe appears at the three-month position, halfway down the side. A face that is looking forward (toward the right edge of the cup handle) appears halfway around the cup.(See Figure 4-4.)

Analyze the cup: Look up *Padlock, Horseshoe,* and *Face.* The padlock indicates trouble is subsiding. The horseshoe indicates good fortune. The face looking forward means you can look forward to a life of achievement.

Interpretation: About six weeks from now, your troubles will suddenly subside and you will have several weeks of peace. Sometime in April, probably around mid-April, you will have some outstanding good fortune. The cup doesn't show exactly what sort of good fortune, but it will not be minor. The horseshoe always brings something major and good into your life.

About mid-year your life will shape up to the place where you will be able to look forward to a life of achievement from that point on. We can infer that perhaps the good fortune you experienced in April had something to do with this turn of events. We can also infer that you have reached a point of wisdom and maturity that enables you to begin a life of achievement

This is a good cup. It promises much for you. Good luck.

To Answer a Question

Use the glossary exactly the same as for a present time reading. The difference is that you interpret the symbols in relation to the question you are answering. The time divisions in the cup (as shown in Figure 3-1, page 12) are not valid.

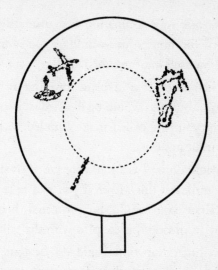

FIGURE 4-5: Cup for Example of Answering a Question

Example of Answering a Question

Question: What sort of work/career is best for me?

Symbols in the cup: A pencil by itself. A coiled snake coupled with an airplane. A guitar coupled with a canopy. (See Figure 4-5.)

Analyze the cup: Look up *Pencil, Snake, Airplane, Guitar,* and *Canopy.* Under *Pencil* it says, "See Pen," which pertains to any occupation concerned with written communication. Under *Snake* it says that a coiled snake is a highly negative sign that pertains to treachery. The airplane refers to travel. The guitar pertains to being a singer or solo performer. The canopy refers to protection.

Interpretation: Any occupation that primarily involves written communications would be good for you (the pencil by itself indicates this).

Any occupation that involves traveling or the transportation business would be disastrous, even dangerous, for you (the coiled snake coupled with the airplane indicates this).

You would do well as a solo entertainer or singer (the guitar indicates this). Even if you had to travel as an entertainer you would be protected because the canopy (protection) is coupled with the guitar.

Any writing occupation would also be good provided it didn't involve traveling or transportation. Some occupations that would be best are creative writer, secretary, court reporter, newspaper reporter (local, not international where traveling is required), copywriter, songwriter, solo entertainer, technical writer for a company, speech writer, and so forth.

Some occupations that would not be advisable are pilot, truck driver, travel agent, working on a ship, airplane, or train, or a traveling salesperson, etc.

Remember, a cup that is used to answer a question can answer only that question. The cup is not valid for other questions or for present time readings.

For a Past Time Reading

Read and interpret the same as for a present time reading except that the time divisions in the cup (shown in Figure 3-1, page 12) are not valid. The time is only relative.

A cup prepared for a past time reading is not valid for use in present time or question answering readings.

FIGURE 4-6: Cup for Example of a Past Lifetime

Example of a Past Lifetime Interpretation

Symbols in the cup: A boat coupled to the letter "F" coupled to a fish. A short distance later there is a coffin coupled to a pool of water coupled to the numeral "1." (See Figure 4-6.)

Analyze the cup: Look up *Boat, Alphabetic Letter, Fish, Coffin,* and *Water*. All you can tell about time is that the coffin, water, and numeral appear later in the cup than the other symbols.

Interpretation: In a previous life you were a fisherman and you died while fishing. Do you see how this interpretation was obtained?

The letter "F" coupled to both the boat and the fish cause them to be interpreted literally. The "F" stands for the activity. Hence, a fisherman in a boat in water. The coffin indicates death, and the water coupled with the numeral causes the water to be interpreted literally. The result is that you probably died in the water while performing your occupation.

Concluding Remarks

A Word About "Seeing" Symbols

You have probably gazed at the clouds in the sky and seen various figures. "There's a horse!" "Look at the chariot!" "Doesn't that look like a whale to you?"

Cloud gazing was a fun pastime as a child. After forty-seven years of marriage, my wife and I still do cloud gazing. I'll bet you do, too, from time to time.

Studying the patterns of tea leaves in a cup is quite similar to cloud gazing. Tea leaves are easy because they don't keep moving like clouds do.

Take your time when you study the tea leaf patterns. Turn the cup around. Tilt it. Turn it upside down. Examine it from all angles.

Allow your imagination to let you see the tea patterns just as you do when you look at cloud patterns. Don't try to force the patterns to be there. The symbols will be quite clear.

Don't expect all of the tea leaves to give you a meaningful symbol. Many of the tea leaves will be just meaningless blobs of wet tea.

I have had some tea cups that had very few symbols in them. They were mostly "blobs." That is okay and is to be expected. It indicates that the forthcoming year will be an ordinary year with little or nothing unusual or different about it—status quo, so to speak. In that sense, the tea leaves do give a meaningful message.

When a symbol is there, it sort of jumps into your awareness. It is clear, and you have no doubt that it is a bee, or an owl, a wagon, or whatever.

Most beginning tea leaf readers who claim to see nothing in the tea cup are usually rushing instead of taking their time. Examining a tea cup is not like watching television. The pictures don't just float into your mind with no effort on your part.

Just take your time. Relax. Pretend you are looking at the clouds or at ink blots to see what you can see. The symbols (pictures) are there.

Some people have more difficulty in "seeing" or "visualizing" than others do. If you are one of these people, you may find it advantageous to use a crystal to help you (see the Appendix for information on using crystals to enhance your ability to read tea leaves). If you are really a "stubborn" non-visualizer, I recommend my audio cassette tape *Psychic Workout* (Llewellyn Publications), which contains a complete creative visualization program. This tape will arouse your innate creative visualization abilities from their sleep and enable you to use them.

Different Kinds of Teas

There are dozens (perhaps hundreds) of different teas on the market that can be used for reading. The most common is orange pekoe, which is the kind found in most tea bags.

Whatever kind you use will work fine. I personally prefer loose (bulk) tea rather than using the contents of a tea bag because I find that bulk tea seems to present clearer and more varied symbols.

Here is something you might want to experiment with: use different teas for different purposes and see what results you get. For example, someone wants you to read their tea leaves to see if there will be any "love in their life," or some other question relating to romance, in the upcoming twelve months. Use a rose hip-blend tea to answer the question.

Perhaps a mint tea will help you answer financial questions, and so forth. You will develop your own techniques and methods.

You might want to read books about herbs and spices to help you select which kind of tea blend to use for specific kinds of readings. Try it. I think you will be amazed at what happens, and I know you will have fun.

The examples given in this chapter should help you get the idea of how to interpret the symbols you see in the tea cup.

In an actual tea leaf reading session, the cup will most likely contain many more symbols than I've used in these few examples. It wouldn't be unusual to see at least a dozen symbols.

I've seen cups that were so loaded with symbols that it took me an hour to interpret them, and I've seen cups that had only two or three symbols.

No matter how many or how few symbols are in the cup, the approach to interpretation is exactly the same as I've given in the examples. Use your common sense and knowledge to fill in additional information just as I did in Examples #2 and #4.

Remember this: there are no unimportant symbols in a tea cup. Only important things will show up in a cup.

Symbol Glossary

This glossary contains nearly 400 commonly seen symbols with comprehensive interpretations for each. Many symbols contain several possible meanings depending on the rest of the cup (i.e., whether it is a man or a woman's cup), and on the physical orientation of the symbol.

Obviously, there are many thousands of possible symbols that might appear in a cup. It isn't reasonably possible to list them all. This glossary contains the ones you are most likely to encounter. It is unlikely you will encounter a symbol such as a coal miner's drill or mariner's sextant, etc. If you do, you should have learned enough from this book to make your own interpretation.

The interpretations given in this glossary may not necessarily be the only possible interpretations. If you have a distinct feeling about a different interpretation when you encounter a symbol, use your interpretation and keep a record to see if it was accurate. This is how you learn and expand your knowledge.

In all likelihood, this glossary will contain ninety-nine percent of everything you will ever need to know.

Unless otherwise stated, all interpretations apply to all three kinds of tea leaf readings—present, past, and question answering.

This glossary furnishes four types of information for each symbol:

Narrative description: Furnishes more detail about interpretation and various shades of meaning.

Key words: For quick reference and general meaning.

Polarity: Positive or negative. Aids you in interpreting symbols that are coupled—that is, within a quarter-inch of each other.

Literal meaning: Specifies when to interpret a symbol literally and when not to.

-*A*-

ACE OF SPADES: This is the shape found on the ace of spades card from an ordinary playing card deck. There are three different interpretations depending on how the symbol is lying in the cup:

Pointing up: If the point of the ace of spades is pointing toward the top of the cup, it indicates trouble or, most commonly, a quarrel. Whatever the trouble or quarrel, it will be disruptive enough to upset your life considerably, but usually for only a short period of time. It is never life threatening or gravely serious by itself.

If the symbol is closely coupled with a highly negative symbol such as a coiled snake, then the trouble could be potentially grave. Closely coupled means that both symbols are within a quarter inch of each other in the cup. The closer together, the stronger the influence of one on the other.

On the other hand, if this symbol is coupled to a heart-shaped symbol, it indicates a lover's quarrel that will likely blow over in a few days (two weeks at most).

Pointing down: If the point of the ace of spades is pointing toward the bottom of the cup, it indicates trouble is subsiding. If the ace is not closely coupled with another symbol, then whatever problem you were having at the time will go away. For example, if the ace is coupled with a dollar sign, your financial troubles will lessen.

Lying across the cup: If the ace is lying across the cup pointing in either direction, it indicates you are now out of danger, usually from an illness. If the ace is not coupled with another sign, then it refers to a recovery from a personal illness.

If this ace is coupled with the symbol of a person of the opposite sex, then it indicates recovery from illness of your closest friend of the opposite sex. If this ace is coupled with the symbol of a dog, it indicates recovery from an illness of your pet, and so on.

Key words for all: Pointing up—quarrel (short-termed). Pointing down—trouble lessening. Lying across—out of danger from an illness.

Polarity for all: Positive.

Literal meaning for all: The ace of spades is never interpreted literally as being an ace of spades.

ACORN: An acorn always indicates multiplication or bounty of some sort. By itself, it indicates general prosperity in your life.

If coupled with a dollar sign, it indicates that your financial situation will improve considerably, usually through investments or savings. If coupled with a baby, it indicates great creativity. Any symbol coupled with an acorn will furnish details concerning the specific way in which you will prosper.

Key words: Productivity. Multiplication. Bountiful.
Polarity: Positive.
Literal meaning: Never interpreted literally.

AIRPLANE: An airplane indicates a trip, usually long distance, i.e., over 300 miles. It applies to all trips, not just trips by air. If the airplane is alone (not coupled with any other  symbol) the trip will be safe, uneventful, routine, and moderately enjoyable.

If the airplane is coupled with any positive symbol, the trip will be exceptionally enjoyable.

If the airplane is coupled with any negative symbol, the trip will be boring, uncomfortable, and fraught with minor problems.

If the airplane seems to be crashing or falling apart, then it would be wise to not take a trip at the time indicated because there is danger of injury or death.

In a past life reading, the crashing airplane would indicate when an injury or death did occur during travel.

Key words: Long distance travel. Danger during travel if the airplane seems to be crashing or falling apart.
Polarity: Positive.
Literal meaning: If an airplane is coupled with a numeral or a letter of the alphabet, interpret the symbol literally as being an airplane.

ALLIGATOR: An alligator indicates survival or longevity. This is a good sign because it indicates you will overcome whatever difficulties life may hand you. While it does generally indicate a long life, it does not necessarily mean a healthy life.

If the alligator is coupled with any positive symbol, there is a reasonably good chance that your life will be healthy.

If coupled with a negative symbol, you will probably have poor health in the later years of your life.

Key words: Survival. Longevity.

Polarity: Positive.

Literal meaning: The alligator is never interpreted literally as being an alligator.

ANCHOR: There are two meanings to the anchor symbol, depending on how it appears in the cup: hanging or lying.

Hanging in midair: This is an unsettled condition. Some aspect of your life is unsettled and frustrating. If the anchor is closely coupled with another symbol, you can determine exactly what is unsettled. For example, with a heart shape, an unsettled love affair; with a dollar sign, unsettled finances. If the anchor is by itself, then it indicates a general unsettled condition in your life that probably affects more than one aspect.

Lying across the cup: A lying anchor indicates that you have reached your destination or goal. If coupled with an anvil symbol, the lying anchor indicates you will reach your work goal at the time indicated in the cup. The destination or goal could be virtually anything: a trip, a work goal, a health destination (better or terminal), etc. Look for other symbols in the cup to help decide what the lying anchor implies.

Key words for all: Hanging anchor—unsettled condition. Lying anchor—destination or goal.
Polarity for all: Positive.
Literal meaning for all: Never interpreted literally.

ANGEL: An angel is one of the best symbols to find in a cup because it assures protection from all negative influences. If the symbol is not coupled with any other symbol, it indicates protection in every aspect of your life. It also indicates that you will likely have a spiritual awakening or awareness at the time indicated in the cup.

If the angel is coupled with another symbol, then interpret it accordingly. For example, if coupled with a crashing airplane, it indicates that you will have an accident while traveling but you will not be hurt.

The polarity of nearby symbols does not affect the angel. The angel's power prevails.

Key words: Protection. Spiritual awareness.
Polarity: Highly positive.
Literal meaning: If the angel is coupled with a numeral or a letter of the alphabet, interpret the angel literally as being an angel.

ANT: An ant indicates achievement. Usually this applies to success in business but also to hobbies, or any endeavor that requires work and dedication.

More than one ant indicates work and success in more than one endeavor if the ants are in different parts of the cup. If the ants are in the same part of the cup, it then indicates a great deal of work in one endeavor with resulting great success. For example, if you saw a cluster of ants at the six-month time segment of the cup, you would say, "In approximately six months you will be extremely busy with hard work, and your efforts will pay off successfully."

If the ant is coupled with a house symbol, the work will be done at home, perhaps building a house, operating a business in the home, remodeling your home, etc. If the ant is coupled with the negative symbol of an earring, all your hard work will not pay off. It will be lost.

Key words: Work. Achievement. Industry. Success, unless coupled with negative symbols indicating otherwise.

Polarity: Positive.

Literal meaning: Never interpreted literally.

ANTELOPE: An antelope signifies a new experience or adventure. Unless this symbol is coupled with some negative symbol, it always indicates a good, enjoyable experience. For example, if coupled with an airplane it indicates an exciting trip to someplace you've never been before. The antelope never indicates a repeat of some experience; it is always something new.

Key words: New experience or adventure.
Polarity: Positive.
Literal meaning: Never interpreted literally.

ANVIL: The anvil indicates work, labor, or service. The usual interpretation is in terms of your job. If coupled with the antelope symbol, it means that you will be getting a new job at the time indicated in the cup.

If it is coupled with a bear, interpret it to mean that you will have to "bear up" under a heavy work load.

Key words: Work. Labor. Service.
Polarity: Positive.
Literal meaning: Never interpreted literally.

APE: An ape means to copy, mimic, duplicate, or (in the negative sense) to steal by copying. For example, if you are a writer and an ape symbol in your cup is coupled with a highly negative symbol such as a coiled snake, it indicates that someone is copying your work without authorization (violation of your copyright).

An ape that is not coupled with another symbol always indicates "you"; that is, you often copy other people rather than be original. For example, an ape by itself could indicate that you follow conventional dress styles so you won't be criticized by others.

Key words: Copy. Mimic. Duplicate.
Polarity: Positive.
Literal meaning: Never interpreted literally.

APPLE: An apple symbol indicates that you will be faced with a temptation at the time indicated in the cup. These temptations are not the casual kind such as whether or not to eat fattening food. An apple refers to a major temptation such as cheating on your mate, stealing from your employer because you are reasonably sure that no one would ever know, spending money on something that you really can't afford, accepting a "tempting" new job offer, etc.

If the apple has a bite taken out of it, then the temptation will definitely be harmful to you if you give in to it. If it doesn't have a bite taken out of it, it could still be harmful to you, but not as disastrous as if the apple has a bite taken out of it.

A whole apple could be a good temptation, or it could be one that will be harmful but not disastrous.

As with all symbols, if the apple is coupled to another symbol, you must blend the meanings to get a more complete interpretation.

Key words: Temptation.
Polarity: Neutral.
Literal meaning: Never interpreted literally.

ARM: An arm has one of three meanings depending on how it is positioned in the cup: extending up, straight out or hanging down.

Extending up: An arm extending upward toward the top of the cup indicates pleading, prayer, asking for help, asking a question, or searching for major answers in some aspect of your life.

If the arm is not coupled with some other symbol, the upward arm usually signifies that you are searching diligently for some major guidance in your life. For example, it can mean seeking the meaning of life, searching for a better life for yourself, or asking for divine guidance. Such a symbol might indicate that you will join some movement, religion, organization, course of study, etc., at the time period indicated in the cup, which you feel will help you enrich your life.

If coupled with the dollar sign ($), it would mean that you will be seeking financial help, perhaps through a bank loan, at the indicated time.

Extending straight out: This arm, extending predominantly across the cup, not upward or downward, signifies assistance. If the arm has no hand on it, or the hand is closed, you will give assistance to someone or to some organization/cause.

If the arm has an open hand, then you will receive assistance. There are no negative connotations to this symbol regardless of whether it is coupled with negative symbols. Even if coupled with a coiled snake, the interpretation means you will either give or receive assistance (depending on the hand) even though there will be treachery that will try to prevent it.

Hanging downward: This indicates that you will either feel helpless or actually be helpless in some situation. If coupled with some negative symbol, you will actually be helpless in the situation.

If coupled with a positive symbol, you will feel helpless but the situation will turn out okay after you've gone through a period of deep concern.

If the downward arm is all by itself in the cup, you will feel acutely helpless to the point of despair. In this case, by knowing in advance that this is going to happen, you can lessen the effect by deliberate positive mental programming. Keep in mind it is only a feeling, and it will pass if you don't do something foolish to cause a problem.

Key words for all: Extending upward—seeking, pleading, searching. Extending straight out—giving or receiving assistance. Hanging downward—helplessness.

Polarity for all: Positive.

Literal meaning for all: If the arm is coupled with a numeral or a letter of the alphabet, interpret the arm literally as being an arm.

ARROW: An arrow indicates that you will find the right direction in some aspect of your life.

If the arrow points upward, the outlook for your life will be much brighter and more rewarding than you had anticipated.

If the arrow points across the cup, the direction of your life will be about what you expected.

If the arrow points downward, the direction you take will be lower than your previous expectations. For example, suppose you had been undecided on which of two people to marry. In your cup you find a ring alongside an arrow. This indicates that you will decide (i.e., find the right direction) on who to marry. The direction of the arrow will indicate how that marriage will match up to your previous expectations.

Key words: Direction you wish to take. The orientation indicates the outcome versus your expectations.

Polarity: Positive.

Literal meaning: Never interpreted literally.

AXE: The axe is always a symbol of danger. The axe always refers to you (the one whose cup is being read) unless it is coupled with some symbol that indicates another person such as a horse, or the figure of a person.

The danger is a physical danger unless another symbol says otherwise. For example, if the axe is coupled with the figure of a woman, some woman you know well (not just casually) will be in physical danger at the time indicated.

If the axe is coupled with a dollar sign, your money or possessions will be in danger at the time indicated.

Key word: Danger.
Polarity: Negative.
Literal meaning: Never interpreted literally.

-B-

BABY: A baby in a cup is always good even when coupled with neg-ative symbols. Negative symbols can indicate problems or difficul-ties, but the "baby" will always triumph. The baby is creativity. This indicates new, fresh, creative ideas and ventures; a fresh start, another chance.

The baby always refers to the person whose cup is being read, never to someone else. If a baby is coupled with a horse (friend), it indicates a new venture with a friend, not merely a friend's new venture; you are always involved.

Key words: New, fresh, creative ideas. New ventures. Fresh start. Another chance.
Polarity: Highly positive.
Literal meaning: If a baby is coupled with a numeral or a letter of the alphabet, interpret the baby literally.

BABY BUGGY (STROLLER):
This signifies either the birth or conception of a child. The time area of the cup indicates when the birth or conception will take place. If you want a child and haven't been able to conceive, try diligently during the period where the baby buggy appears in your tea cup; you will succeed.

Key words: Birth or conception of a child.
Polarity: Positive.
Literal meaning: Never interpreted literally.

BAG: The symbol of a bag in your tea cup indicates that you are going to get something. You will get something important, not just a trivial gift. Most often it indicates you will get something on the order of a new job, a raise, or relief from financial stress. The bag always pertains to you, not to someone else.

If the bag is coupled with another symbol, it will give you a better idea of exactly what you will get.

Key words: Receive. Obtain.
Polarity: Positive.
Literal meaning: Never interpreted literally.

BALL: Interpret a ball in your cup as a smooth-going period in your life and activities during the time indicated. Whatever you plan during that period will happen regardless of who or what may try to prevent it. You will just "roll on" with your activities without being impeded.

The ball symbol is always interpreted by itself, never coupled with other symbols. It does not necessarily bring with it good luck, only unimpeded progress. The progress could turn out to be unlucky. For this reason, be sure to exercise sound judgment in your words and actions during this period because you will make progress. If your progress is driven by faulty judgment or lack of integrity, you will likely have disastrous results.

Key words: Smooth going. Unimpeded progress.
Polarity: Positive.
Literal meaning: Never interpreted literally.

BALLOON: There are two different kinds of balloons, each with its own unique interpretation. One is a party balloon on a string such as a child might play with. The other is a hot air balloon that carries passengers and soars to high altitudes.

Party balloon: A party balloon indicates a good time, a celebration, a party, fun. By itself, not coupled with some other nearby symbol, the party balloon simply means you will be having a good time, perhaps at a party in your honor, etc. If there is a closely coupled symbol, then you must blend the meanings together. For example, if the party balloon is next to a bee, your celebration will trigger gossip. If next to a dollar sign, it will be a costly party.

Hot air balloon: The hot air balloon indicates taking a chance, a risk. If the balloon is not coupled with another symbol, then the time period will be one where you find yourself taking many chances. These chances could be good or bad, or a mixture of the two.

There is nothing wrong with taking a chance if it doesn't involve the potential for harm to yourself or to others. For example, purchasing a one-dollar state lottery ticket is "taking a chance." No real harm done. However, speeding on an ice-coated highway is also "taking a chance," but it quite possibly could involve harm to yourself or to others.

During this period of time you need to exercise extra sound judgment because you will be inclined to want to throw caution to the wind and take a chance.

If the hot air balloon is coupled with a negative symbol, it is a stern warning of serious danger. If coupled with a positive symbol, your risk-taking will likely be beneficial. For example, if a four-leaf clover is next to a hot air balloon, you'd be well advised to purchase some lottery tickets at that time.

Key words for all: Party balloon—fun, celebration, party, good time. Hot air balloon—a chance, risk.
Polarity for all: Positive.
Literal meaning for all: Never interpreted literally.

BANANA: A banana signifies a foreign country. It usually means that you will receive news from a foreign country, probably by a letter. If it is a bunch of bananas, then you will be communicating back and forth with someone in a foreign country more than once.

If the banana is coupled with another symbol, then blend the two meanings to obtain a more detailed interpretation. For example, if a banana is next to an airplane, you will be traveling to a foreign country during the time period indicated in the cup.

Key words: Foreign communications.
Polarity: Neutral.
Literal meaning: Never interpreted literally.

BANISTER: The banister means friendship. During the time indicated in the cup, you will be involved in some significant way in a friendship. This could be meeting a new friend who will play an important role in your life. It could mean you will befriend someone in some important way. It could mean that an existing friendship takes on a deeper, fuller meaning. In any case, it will be a period in which you will be acutely aware of friendship, and friendship will play an important role in your life at that time.

If the banister is coupled with some other symbol, then blend the two to obtain a more specific interpretation. For example, a banister coupled with a heart shape would indicate that a friend could also become a lover.

Key word: Friendship.
Polarity: Positive.
Literal meaning: Never interpreted literally.

BARN: A barn indicates an abundance of material goods. Most commonly, it refers to an abundance of food but it also applies to other material goods.
It does not mean money unless it is coupled with some other symbols that signify money.

Key words: Abundance. Plenty. Material goods only. Not spiritual. Not money (except as noted above).

Polarity: Positive.

Literal meaning: If a barn is coupled with a numeral or a letter of the alphabet, interpret the barn literally.

BARREL: The interpretation of barrel depends on whether the barrel is full or empty.

Empty barrel: This indicates a serious lack of something in your life. You could be lacking love, security, goals, money, food, or virtually anything. If it is coupled with another symbol, you can get a clearer picture of specifically what is lacking.

An empty barrel can also be a warning to you to not become obsessed with what you lack to the point where you allow it to affect your thoughts or actions in a negative direction. The way to deal effectively with an empty barrel in a cup is to maintain a positive attitude and to act with integrity. Otherwise, you can lead yourself into a downward spiral to "the bottom of the barrel" and become less of a person than you are capable of being.

Full barrel: This indicates a period of time in which you can increase your worth, spiritually and materially, if you are willing to work for it. The full barrel does not give you a free ride to prosperity, but it does give you the opportunity to fill out your life if you take positive action to do so.

Key words for all: Empty barrel—serious lack in your life. A warning about your attitude. Full barrel—opportunity for increasing your life materially and spiritually. You must work for it. No free rides.

Polarity for all: Neutral.

Literal meaning for all: Never interpreted literally.

BASKET: The interpretation of a basket in your cup depends on whether the basket is full or empty.

Full basket: A full basket means you will receive recognition in some way. It could mean that you receive a compliment from someone important to you. It could also mean receiving an honor or award for something you have done. It will be something more significant than someone merely saying, "You look nice today." If it is a compliment, it will be something like your boss saying to her boss in your presence, "(your name) is one of our outstanding employees, and I want to see them given a more responsible position in the company." The full basket is not trivial—it signifies recognition in some important way.

Empty basket: The empty basket indicates depression, your mental depression. The depression is temporary and will quickly pass unless the empty basket is coupled with some negative symbol. In this case, the depression could be serious and you may need to seek professional help to handle it.

Polarity for all: Neutral.
Literal meaning for all: Never interpreted literally.

BAT: This is the mammal, not a baseball bat. The bat is a negative symbol. Even if not coupled with another symbol, the  bat will bring treachery into your life.

The treachery is always from another person, and that person usually is not someone you would think of as your friend. Most often, the treachery will come from someone you either don't know or know only casually.

By itself, the bat is not life threatening, but it will still cause you considerable trouble. If the bat is coupled with another negative symbol, such as a coiled snake, there is a potential for a life-threatening situation.

"Forewarned is half armed." If you know in advance that this is a hazardous period for you, you can take precautions to protect yourself and to lessen the danger. You can even prevent the treachery from materializing if you are diligent in your actions and precautions. For example, suppose you are a woman and you work the night shift in a convenience store. During this period, arrange to be escorted to and from work every night by one or two male companions. Arrange to have one or two male companions with you 100 percent of the time at work, either in the store or parked in front where they can see everything. I know this sounds like overreaction, but the bat symbol in a cup is that threatening.

Fortunately, a bat is rarely seen in a cup. Of course, if the bat is coupled with a positive symbol, then the threat becomes much less dangerous. The positive symbol will downgrade the problem to a "close call" or a merely frightening one with no physical harm done.

Key words: Treachery. Serious danger. Might pose a life-threatening situation.

Polarity: Highly negative.

Literal meaning: Never interpreted literally.

BATHTUB: The bathtub signifies that you have need for either improved personal hygiene or for spiritual cleansing. It may mean that you have offensive body odor and need to wash more thoroughly and use a deodorant. It also signifies that you need to pay closer attention to the cleansing of your private parts.

If the bathtub is coupled with a negative symbol, then your hygiene problem is (or potentially can be) responsible for some physical ailment such as itching, sores, discharges.

If your physical hygiene is fine, then the bathtub indicates a need for spiritual cleansing. You should tend to this as soon as you can in accordance with your personal beliefs.

If the bathtub is coupled with a negative symbol, then your spiritual situation is such that it can cause you serious mental problems, such as depression, if not attended to.

Key words: Need for improved personal hygiene. Need for spiritual cleansing.

Polarity: Negative.

Literal meaning: Never interpreted literally.

BEACON LIGHT: The beacon light is a very positive symbol that promises you increased spiritual development, enlightenment, awareness, and understanding. Literally, you will be shown the way to conduct your life in a more fulfilling, enjoyable, and satisfying manner.

If the beacon light is coupled with a negative symbol, it has the power to nearly eradicate the effects of the negative symbol. For example, if the beacon light was coupled with a bat in your cup, the powerful threat posed by the bat could be reduced to a close call that you may not even be aware of.

Key words: Spiritual development. Enlightenment. Awareness. Understanding. Negating effect on negative symbols.

Polarity: Highly positive.

Literal meaning: Never interpreted literally.

BEAR: The bear is a powerful symbol. It can be either positive or negative depending on its demeanor in the cup: ferocious, gentle, or playful.

Ferocious bear: If the bear appears to be ferocious or attacking, snarling, etc., in the cup, then it is a danger signal. The bear, if not coupled with a strongly negative symbol such as the bat, is never a life-threatening danger. The danger is more in the order of losing money through ill-advised investments; danger of losing your job because of quarrels, misunderstandings, or disagreements with someone on the job; danger of total breakup with your mate or lover due to emotional disagreements.

Gentle bear: A bear that is just standing or walking, and not in a vicious manner, is a powerful positive symbol for personal strength to effectively deal with any situation you may encounter.

This symbol, if coupled with any negative symbol, gives you the physical, mental, and spiritual strength to effectively deal with the negative situation so you will triumph over it. The negative situation may give you some "lumps" physically or emotionally, but it will not deter you.

Playful bear: A bear that seems to be playful, such as sitting up or offering you a paw to shake, indicates powerful help from someone when you need it.

Key words for all: Ferocious—danger. Gentle—personal strength. Playful—help when you need it.

Polarity for all: Ferocious—negative. Gentle or playful—positive.

Literal meaning for all: Never interpreted literally.

BEAVER: The beaver always refers
to constructive activity, usually to
your occupation or to your hobby.
It can also refer to your involvement in a fraternal organization.

During the time period indicated in the cup, you will
be exceptionally busy building your reputation, organization, etc. For example, the person who pursues crafts
as a hobby will be exceptionally busy creating whatever
crafts he or she pursues.

Unless the beaver is coupled with some negative symbol that indicates otherwise, the activity will always be
constructive and rewarding.

Key words: Exceptionally busy. Constructive.
Rewarding.

Polarity: Positive.

Literal meaning: Never interpreted literally.

BED: This is a bed you sleep in, not a flower bed, truck
bed, etc. It can mean either of two things: peace or
forming an alliance. Interpret the bed symbol all by
itself; it does not change due to the proximity of nearby
symbols, whether they are positive or negative.

Peace: During the time period indicated in the cup, you
will feel at peace with yourself and the world. You

may well find a total inner peace that will last for the rest of your life.

Alliance: During the indicated time period, it is likely that you will form some sort of alliance with another person. It could be a marriage, but most often it is an alliance at work or within some organization. For example, you may develop an arrangement between your department and another department to share the workload on some company project in such a way as to save time and money.

Key words for all: Peace. Alliance.

Polarity for all: Positive.

Literal meaning for all: If the bed is coupled with a numeral or alphabetic letter, interpret the bed literally.

BEE: The bee is a negative symbol that rarely causes serious problems, but it always is a nuisance and often destroys friendships.

The bee signifies gossip. During the time period indicated in the cup, you will likely either be gossiping or be gossiped about—or both. Gossiping is an act you can do something about simply by not doing it. There isn't much you can do about someone gossiping about you except to deal with it maturely when the time comes.

Key word: Gossip.

Polarity: Negative.

Literal meaning: Never interpreted literally.

BEEHIVE: The beehive signifies that you will receive an important invitation, most likely one that you weren't expecting.

If the beehive is not coupled with a negative symbol, the invitation is one you can look forward to because it will be enjoyable and beneficial.

If it is coupled with a negative symbol, you need to blend the two to see specifically what may happen. For example, if coupled with a bee, the invitation will generate gossip against you.

Key word: Invitation.

Polarity: Neutral.

Literal meaning: Never interpreted literally.

BEETLE: The beetle (insect) is a good sign to find in your tea cup. By itself, it signifies moderate good fortune in general.

If coupled with a negative symbol, the beetle cancels the effect of the negative symbol.

If coupled with a positive symbol, it brings great good fortune in the area governed by the other symbol. For example, if coupled with a dollar sign ($), it signifies that you will come into a great deal of money during the time period indicated in the cup. If coupled with an anvil, it indicates great good fortune in your work.

Key words: Good fortune.

Polarity: Positive.

Literal meaning: Never interpreted literally.

BELL: The bell relies heavily on being coupled with a nearby symbol in order to determine its meaning. A bell all by itself signifies an announcement but it gives no indication of what. If the bell is coupled with a dollar sign ($), it would indicate an announcement of a salary increase; if coupled with a casket, an announcement of a death; and so on. You will need to look to nearby symbols for the meaning. If there are no nearby symbols, then you are not able to predict anything more than a vague announcement.

Key word: Announcement.
Polarity: Neutral.
Literal meaning: Never interpreted literally.

BICYCLE: The bicycle means that you need to bring more balance into your life. Perhaps you are a workaholic to the detriment of your family. Perhaps you spend an inordinate amount of money on frivolous items instead of paying your bills, etc. Whatever the case, you need to do a serious evaluation of your life situation and conduct and then bring them into balance.

If the bicycle is coupled with a positive symbol, you will have the insight to know exactly what to do to improve your life and bring it into balance.

If the bicycle is coupled with a negative symbol, you will be blind to your own shortcomings, likely blame someone else, and not do anything to improve your situation. You will probably need professional advice to straighten things out. If you decline to seek professional advice, your life will likely be torn apart—a divorce, getting fired from work, or whatever.

If the bicycle is all by itself, you have a 50-50 chance of correcting the situation without professional help.

Key words: Need for balance in your life.
Polarity: Negative.
Literal meaning: If a bicycle is coupled with a numeral or an alphabetic letter, interpret the bicycle literally.

BIRD: A bird is one of the most commonly seen symbols in tea leaves. Often the bird is of a generic type. It is just a bird, of no distinguishable species. The bird is either flying or perched with each having its own interpretation. In addition, there are twelve specific types of birds, each with its own unique meaning. All of these interpretations are included here. *None of the birds are ever interpreted literally.*

Generic perched bird: A perched generic bird is interpreted as "waiting for a message." Usually it indicates that you are in fact waiting for a message (letter, phone call, telegram, etc.) from someone. It is always a message that you consider important. It can also mean that someone is waiting for an overdue message from you if the perched bird is coupled with the symbol of a person.

Key words: Waiting for communication.
Polarity: Neutral.

Generic flying bird: A generic bird in flight indicates that a good message is either in the process of being sent to you or will be shortly.

Key words: Communication is on the way.

Polarity: Neutral.

Duck: A duck always represents false gossip. During the time period indicated in the cup, you will be the object of false gossip.

Key words: False gossip.

Polarity: Slightly negative.

Eagle: The eagle indicates that you will soar over trouble, obstacles, and resistance. An eagle is a good symbol to find in a cup because it promises that you will have whatever it takes to triumph.

Key words: Triumph over troubles, obstacles.

Polarity: Positive.

Goose: A goose always applies to someone you will be dealing with during the time period indicated. That person will be quarrelsome, cranky, and difficult to deal with. It may be someone you currently know or it may be someone new, but whoever it is, they will make life especially unpleasant for you during that period.

Key words: Quarrelsome, difficult person.

Polarity: Negative.

Hen: A hen indicates a talkative person. This is the kind of person who could talk the ears off a statue. This person may be charming, witty, and delightful if coupled with a positive symbol. This person will be a colossal irritant if coupled with a negative symbol. If the hen is alone in the cup, the person will be a bore. In any case, you will have this person imposed on you, and you will have to deal with the situation as you choose.

Key words: A talkative person.

Polarity: Slightly negative.

Owl: The owl is a wise person who will play an important part in your life during the time period. The influence of this wise person will last for the rest of your life. The axiom "When the student is ready, the teacher shall appear" applies here. The owl will be your "teacher." The owl is a very important, positive symbol to have in a cup because it opens the door to your expanded awareness and learning.

Key words: Wisdom. Wise person.

Polarity: Highly positive.

Parrot: The parrot is a person who will tell everything he or she knows. Parrots repeat things. Parrots will not honor a confidence. Parrots tell secrets.

If there is a parrot in your cup, there will be someone in your life that is a parrot. Be discreet about whom you trust. Make sure you know with whom you are dealing. If you are too trusting or naive, you will likely be caused embarrassment or even great difficulty by the "parrot."

Key words: Person who tells everything they know.

Polarity: Negative.

Peacock: The peacock indicates great pride. If coupled with the symbol of a person or a friend (such as a horse), the proud person is not you. Otherwise the peacock refers to you.

If the peacock is coupled with a negative symbol, it means that your pride is out of hand, making you haughty, aloof, self-centered, etc.

If the peacock is coupled with a positive symbol or is all by itself, it indicates that you have a healthy sense of pride in your work, appearance, etc., but you keep your pride in check so that you don't become self-centered.

If the peacock is coupled with a dollar sign ($), it indicates that you squander money on yourself.

Key words: Great pride.

Polarity: Slightly positive.

Pheasant: The pheasant is a timid person with whom you will be interacting. If you take the trouble to cultivate the timid person's friendship, you will gain a valuable friend.

Key words: Timid person.

Polarity: Positive.

Roadrunner: This indicates that you will be receiving important, valuable news very quickly. The communication will be by telephone, telegram, or some other fast means—never by ordinary mail.

Key words: Communication coming very fast.

Polarity: Positive.

Rooster: The rooster is a boastful person whom you will find to be an irritant. Unfortunately the rooster is likely to be a person whose position is such that it wouldn't be prudent for you to cross him or her. It would be wise for you to "grin and bear it," but you probably will never like this person.

Key words: Boastful person. Braggart.

Polarity: Slightly negative.

Turkey: Interpret the turkey as "stupid behavior." It could be your stupid behavior or that of someone else. If the turkey is not coupled with another symbol, then it refers to you. Since you know in advance that you will be inclined to stupid behavior during the indicated period, be doubly vigilant to guard your words and actions. Keep in mind the axiom, "It is better to keep your mouth shut and be thought stupid than to open your mouth and remove all doubts."

Key words: Stupid behavior.

Polarity: Slightly negative.

Vulture: The vulture foretells poverty, deprivation, serious disruption in your financial status and material security. Usually the problem is caused by some person you trusted and who let you down, usually deliberately through deception.

This is a very negative symbol. Like most negative symbols, the dire results will not occur if you act ahead of time to avert the problem. Heed the warning of the vulture, and you can avert disaster.

Key words: Poverty. Deprivation. Serious disruption in your life.

Polarity: Highly negative.

BOAT: A boat in your tea leaves indicates that you will be gaining money, property, or other valuables, usually through an inheritance or from winnings (such as a  lottery or sweepstakes). There are different shades of meanings depending on the kind of boat.

Canoe: canoe indicates a modest amount of money or other valuables will be coming your way, probably less than a thousand dollars.

Ferry: A ferry indicates that you will have to share your inheritance or winnings with a number of other people, thus cutting down on your individual take. It could be either a small or a large amount of money, but you will have to split it with others.

Row boat: A row boat indicates that your inheritance or winnings will be slow in coming, quite possibly spread in payments over some period of time; or, there simply may be some sort of delay before you can get it, such as legal entanglements. You will not get it all at once. The amount may be large or small, but most likely will exceed a thousand dollars.

Ship: This is the big one! You will receive a very large amount of money, and most likely all at once. However, if it is a sailing ship rather than a powered ship, there may be some delay in getting all of it, perhaps through time payments.

Warship: If the ship is definitely a warship, you will have to fight (legally) for your inheritance. There are certain to be legal challenges made against your receiving the inheritance or winnings. Unless the warship is coupled with a positive symbol, you cannot be certain that you will actually gain some or all of your potential inheritance or winnings.

Key words for all: Inheritance. Winnings. Windfall.
Polarity for all: Positive.
Literal meaning for all: If any of the various boats is coupled with a numeral or a letter of the alphabet, interpret the boat literally as being a boat (of whichever type).

BONE: A bone signifies gossip. Multiple bones signify much gossip that persists over a period of time. However, if the bones are crossed or if the bones are part of a skeleton structure, or if it is a "wishbone," this interpretation of gossip does not apply. In these cases, see *Crossed Bones* or *Skeleton* or *Wishbone* elsewhere in this glossary.

There are three different symbols for gossip, each with a slightly different shade of meaning. A "bee" may be either true or false gossip, but it is social gossip. A duck is always false gossip. A bone or bones may be either true or false gossip, but it is always directed at you personally with the intent of damaging or destroying your reputation. Bones are deliberately malicious gossip.

Key words: Malicious gossip.

Polarity: Negative.

Literal meaning: Never interpreted literally.

BOOK: A book in the tea leaves can mean either of two things depending on whether the book is open or closed.

Open book: An open book signifies
revelation, learning, expanding awareness and knowledge. This is a good symbol to have in your cup because it promises that you will progress in your growth as a person and will prepare yourself for greater achievement and experience. It also indicates that you will be open in your dealings with others.

Closed book: A closed book indicates secrecy. You are not completely open in your dealings with others, always holding something back to give you what you think will be an advantage over others. Such behavior also tends to limit your own growth as a person.

Key words for all: Open book—revelation, learning, openness with others. Closed book—secrecy, growth limiting, not completely open with others.

Polarity for all: Open book—positive. Closed book—slightly negative.

Literal meaning for all: If the book is coupled with a numeral or a letter of the alphabet, interpret the book as literally.

BOTTLE: A bottle (not a jug or a jar) indicates temptation. This will always be a temptation to do something that is unwise for you to do.

If the bottle is coupled with some negative symbol, you will pay dearly if you give in to the temptation.

If the bottle is coupled with some positive symbol, you will gain a great deal if you do not give in to the temptation.

If the bottle is by itself, the results of your giving in to the temptation will lie dormant for a long time and then suddenly rear up to haunt you. If the bottle is by itself and you choose to not give in to the temptation, you will immediately gain self-respect.

Key word: Temptation.
Polarity: Neutral.
Literal meaning: Never interpreted literally.

BOW: There are two kinds of bows. One is an archery bow for shooting arrows. The other is the kind of bow you make with ribbon and put on gift packages or in a little girl's hair. Each has a different interpretation from the other. A shoestring bow is interpreted the same as the ribbon bow.

Archery bow: The archery bow indicates that you will make plans for a trip. You will have the money, reservations will have been made, everything will be prepared. If the archery bow does not have an arrow in it, the trip will not materialize. Something out of your control will happen to cancel or delay the trip. If the bow does have an arrow in it, then the trip will happen as planned.

Ribbon bow: This indicates a close friendship. You will meet the person who will become this close friend during the time period in which the bow appears in the tea cup.

Key words for all: Archery bow—planned trip. Ribbon bow—friendship.

Polarity for all: Positive.

Literal meaning for all: Never interpreted literally.

BOWL: The bowl pertains to material status in life. There are two interpretations, depending on whether the bowl is full or empty.

Full bowl: You have plenty of material goods. If the bowl is heaping, then you have more than you really need or appreciate.

Empty bowl: You have a strong desire for more material goods than you have. You may indeed have very little in the way of material goods. However, you may actually have ample material goods, but you are greedy for more. The greed aspect will be present if there is a nearby negative symbol.

Key words for all: Full bowl—plenty of material goods. Empty bowl—you want more material goods than you have.

Polarity for all: Positive.

Literal meaning for all: Never interpreted literally.

BOX: A box always signifies a gift that you will receive. If there are any symbols coupled with the box, you will be able to tell more about the gift or who is giving it.

For example, if a ribbon bow is on or near the box, it will be a gift of friendship. If an anvil is near the box, the gift will have something to do with your work.

The box is always a positive sign even if there are nearby negative symbols. Negative symbols do not influence the gift, they must be interpreted separately in relation to something other than the gift.

Key words: You will receive a gift.

Polarity: Positive.

Literal meaning: Never interpreted literally.

BREAD: Bread pertains to your personal day-to-day sustenance. One slice of bread indicates a difficult period of time for you that will require pinching pennies, prudent spending, cutting back or eliminating luxuries, etc. You will get through the period okay, but not easily.

A loaf of bread indicates a period of prosperity and plenty which you will get through quite easily.

Key words: One slice—difficult period for you with regard to your daily sustenance. A loaf—an easy period of prosperity and plenty.

Polarity: Positive.

Literal meaning: Never interpreted literally.

BRIDE'S DRESS: You will be expecting a great change in your life, but how that change turns out depends on the rest of the cup.

If the bride's dress stands alone in the cup, not coupled with any other symbol, then it signifies a marriage. Usually it means your own marriage, but if you are already married, it signifies a marriage of someone very close to you, and that the marriage will somehow also affect your own life.

If the bride's dress is coupled with another symbol, then you must take into account the effect of the other symbol. For instance, if coupled with a dog it means that a close friend will be getting married. If coupled with a cat, it indicates treachery in your own marriage. If coupled with a carrot, it indicates that marriage offers a great opportunity for you.

The marriage may not necessarily mean matrimony but rather a great change concerned with you joining or embracing a different lifestyle; for example, a new religion, a new job, residing in a new country.

Key words: Great change in your life, usually by marriage but not always with marriage.

Polarity: Neutral.

Literal meaning: Most often it means matrimony, but not always. It does not just mean "bride's dress."

BRIDGE: If the bridge (any kind) is intact, it means one thing; if it has a substantial break in it, it's another. In this symbol do not regard thin cracks as being a break.

Unbroken bridge: This indicates a successful cementing of relations with someone or something. Suppose, for example, that you lacked the required education or training for a job you deeply desired to have. In your cup you saw an unbroken bridge coupled with the symbol of an open book. This would indicate that if you pursue the training, you will be successful in obtaining the job. Another example: Suppose you are having difficulty with your love life and the symbol of a heart is near an unbroken bridge. This indicates that you will overcome your love problems and have a successful relationship with the object of your love.

If the bridge does not have a nearby symbol to define what problem you will be bridging, then the bridge means that you will be successful in overcoming whatever problem you are having at the time indicated in the cup.

An unbroken bridge is always a good symbol to have because it indicates that you will find the means to overcome whatever is causing you a problem.

Broken bridge: This indicates that your efforts to overcome your problem will not be successful at the time period indicated.

The broken bridge is not necessarily permanent; that is, your efforts will not pay off in the time period indicated in the cup, but they possibly may bear fruit at some later time.

If the broken bridge is coupled with some negative symbol, then your efforts in regard to that specific problem will never be successful. If coupled to a positive symbol, your efforts will likely pay off eventually, but not immediately.

If the broken bridge is by itself in the tea cup, then the outcome could go either way.

Key words for all: Unbroken bridge—successfully overcoming a problem at that time. Broken bridge—unsuccessful at overcoming a problem at that time.

Polarity for all: Neutral.

Literal meaning for all: If a bridge is coupled with a numeral or a letter, interpret the symbol literally.

BROOM: A broom is interpreted as a new home. It usually means you will be either purchasing or moving into a new home during the time period indicated in the cup. A new home does not necessarily mean that it will be a newly constructed home. It may well be a home that has been previously owned by someone else. However, it will be a new home to you.

As with most symbols, other symbols can often give you additional details about the home if those symbols are close enough to be regarded as coupled. Recall from earlier in this book that "coupled" means that the adjacent symbol must be within a quarter-inch away.

Key words: New home.

Polarity: Positive.

Literal meaning: Never interpreted literally.

BRUSH: There are two kinds of brushes considered here—hairbrushes and paintbrushes. Each kind has its own unique interpretation. The paintbrush may be the kind you use to paint a house or to paint pictures—the interpretation is the same.

Hairbrush: This is a personal symbol. It means that you need to pay closer attention to your personal grooming. This means not only your hair, but also body cleanliness, clothing, breath, and general appearance.

This symbol usually doesn't appear in a cup unless you are quite socially unacceptable in your physical care. The only time the hairbrush pertains to someone other than yourself is when the brush is coupled with one of the symbols that indicates another person (horse, figure of a person, etc.).

The implication of the appearance of a hairbrush in your cup is that you will not succeed beyond where you are at the present time unless you improve your appearance substantially.

Paintbrush: The paintbrush pertains to your personal property—house, car, equipment, furnishings, etc. The paintbrush indicates that you need to keep your personal property in better condition than you do. The implication of a paintbrush in your cup is that you will face considerable expense if you don't do a better job of maintaining what you own.

Key words for all: Hairbrush—you need to tend to your personal grooming. Paintbrush—you need to tend to the maintenance of your personal property.

Polarity for all: Negative.

Literal meaning for all: Never interpreted literally.

BUFFALO: A buffalo means "independent" or "force." It is difficult to know which of the two possible interpretations to give when the buffalo is not coupled with another symbol. I lean toward the interpretation of "independent" because I find it to be most often accurate.

The buffalo indicates that you need to act independently; that is, do not rely on someone else to help you or do it for you. You must do it yourself.

If the buffalo is coupled with an unbroken bridge, then I would interpret the buffalo as "force"; that is, you will succeed in overcoming your problem only if you act in a forceful manner.

The buffalo is one symbol with which you will need to exercise your own judgment. Keep records and see what interpretation works best for you.

Key words: Independent. Force.
Polarity: Positive.
Literal meaning: Never interpreted literally.

BULL: The bull is definitely "force," unless coupled with a symbol that indicates money. When coupled with money, the bull means "bull market."

The bull means you must act forcefully against any adversity or opposition if you want to win or succeed. When there is a bull in your cup, you cannot take a "wait and see" attitude about anything. If you do, the world will pass you by without giving you any notice.

In life there are times when it is prudent to keep a low profile, but not when there is a bull symbol in your cup. Make yourself known and be noticed. If you do, things will work out well for you.

This doesn't mean that you should be a bully or behave in an antagonistic manner. Quite the contrary. You must display steady, confident, dignified strength and not back down from any opposition.

Key words: Force. Forceful behavior. Strength.
Polarity: Positive.
Literal meaning: Never interpreted literally.

BUSH: The bush indicates something hidden from your understanding. There is something important that you are unable to comprehend or see through.

If the bush seems to be burning, or if fire is closely coupled with the bush, then you will receive a spiritual experience that will enlighten you.

Other closely coupled symbols will help you to understand more details about what it is you are unable to understand. For example, if coupled with a heart, a love situation; if with an anvil, something to do with your work, and so forth.

If the bush is by itself, then you will have general confusion in your life during the indicated period of time.

Key words: Something hidden from your understanding. Possible spiritual experience. Confusion.

Polarity: Neutral.

Literal meaning: Never interpreted literally.

BUTTERFLY: This powerful symbol indicates a significant change in your life that will start to take place at the time indicated by its placement in the cup. This is a major change, one that will turn your life completely around. This is the kind of change that alters the entire rest of your life—there is no turning back to the way it used to be.

The butterfly is neutral. It indicates a major change but does not indicate what kind of change. It does not couple with other symbols; that is, the polarity and nature of other symbols do not influence the butterfly or vice versa. In my experience, the butterfly indicates a beneficial change more often than not. The change usually is negative only when you fight the change rather than flow harmoniously with it.

Here are two hypothetical examples that illustrate the magnitude of change foretold by a butterfly symbol:

1. You are an agnostic or an atheist. Then one day you have an experience that impels you to turn to religion, perhaps even becoming a clergy member in that religion.

2. You have an experience that awakens your innate psychic ability, and you become a practicing psychic, solving crimes, finding missing persons, healing, etc.

Key words: Major, irreversible change in your life.
Polarity: Neutral.
Literal meaning: Never interpreted literally.

-C-

CABBAGE: There is something "fishy" (not quite on the up and up) with some person, deal or arrangement that you will be involved in.

This is a warning to take your time and investigate thoroughly any personal involvement or any prospective business deals during the time period indicated. If you look closely, you will most likely find the flaws and save yourself a lot of trouble. If you ignore the warning, you will most likely have a lot of problems and regrets.

Key words: Hidden flaws in people or business deals.
Polarity: Negative.
Literal meaning: Never interpreted literally.

CAMEL: A camel indicates endurance and persever-ance. You will overcome your problems and achieve your goals during the time period because you will have the endurance and perseverance required to triumph.

If it is a one-hump camel, it will be difficult for you, but you will still have what it takes to overcome your problems. If a two-hump camel, you will triumph easily.

Key words: Endurance. Perseverance.
Polarity: Positive.
Literal meaning: Never interpreted literally.

CANDLE: There are different shades of meaning depending on whether the candle is lit or unlit.

Lit candle: Indicates that just when things look the dark-est for you, someone or some event will show you the way.

Not lit: You will be shown the way, but not just yet. The unlit candle means you still have some lessons to learn, some experiences to go through before you will see the "light," so to speak.

In either case, however, you will eventually be shown the way. You won't have to wait long. The lit candle will show you the way during the time period indicated. The unlit candle will show you the way within two to six months after the time shown.

Key words for all: You will be shown the way.
Polarity for all: Positive.
Literal meaning for all: Never interpreted literally.

CANE: A cane indicates that you will need some sort of assistance during the time indicated in the cup. Usually it will be because you have a temporary illness, although it could be for some other problem such as finances or a project.

If the cane is coupled with some other symbol, you should be able to get a clearer story. For example, coupled with a dollar sign, it means you will need financial help.

If the cane is coupled with any positive sign, you will receive all the help you need, and if the cane is by itself you will receive some help.

If the cane is coupled with any negative symbol you will not receive the help you need and will have to handle the problem by yourself.

Key words: You will need assistance, usually because of a temporary illness.
Polarity: Negative.
Literal meaning: Never interpreted literally.

CANOPY: A canopy is a symbol of protection. You will be protected from all harm during the time period indicated in the cup. Even if the canopy is coupled with negative symbols, you will not be harmed.

The negative symbols may make you uncomfortable or cause you concern, but no harm will come. For example, suppose a cat is coupled with the canopy. Someone would try to harm you, perhaps by lying about you, but they won't succeed. You will be okay. You may get angry about it, but that is about the extent of it.

Key words: You are protected.
Polarity: Positive.
Literal meaning: Never interpreted literally.

CANTEEN: The canteen signifies a sharing friendship. In the time period indicated, you will find yourself in a situation where you will be sharing something with someone else. It may be with someone you don't currently know or it may be with someone you've known for some time.

More often than not, the sharing will be with someone who is currently a stranger but who will become a friend. It could be as simple as sharing a taxicab on a rainy day when cabs are hard to get. It could be as profound as sharing a spiritual experience that draws you together, such as sharing a table in an overcrowded restaurant, or sharing bus fare because one of you didn't have it, and so forth. There are literally thousands of situations that could occur. What will occur is a bond between you and the other person or persons.

If a canteen is coupled with any negative symbol, it means that some unpleasant circumstance causes you to be in the sharing situation. The negative influence, however, does not affect the relationship between you and the other person. That relationship will be good, friendly, and probably long lasting.

Key words: Sharing friendship.
Polarity: Positive.
Literal meaning: Never interpreted literally.

CAR: A car signifies that you will be taking a trip during the time period in which the car appears. Usually a car indicates domestic travel between 300 and 1,000 miles, although it sometimes indicates longer travel. If you live near another country's border, it could also indicate foreign travel.

If the car is coupled with a positive symbol, it will be an enjoyable, worry-free trip.

If coupled with a negative symbol, the trip will be marred by serious problems. If the car is coupled with a gravely negative symbol such as a snake or a casket, you may want to consider postponing the trip to a different time period. At the very least, take extra precautions if a negative symbol is coupled to the car.

If the car is alone, the trip will be enjoyable and will have only minor problems at most.

Key words: Domestic travel, usually under 1,000 miles.

Polarity: Positive.

Literal meaning: If the car is coupled with a numeral or a letter of the alphabet, interpret it literally as a car.

CARROT: A carrot signifies opportunity. You will have an opportunity presented to you during the time period indicated in the cup.

If the carrot is complete with its leafy top, it will be a great opportunity with much potential. If the carrot does not have its top, it will be an opportunity worth considering but it won't have as great a potential as if the top were present.

If the carrot is coupled with any negative symbol, it means there are hidden factors about the opportunity that you need to address before making your decision. If you ignore the negative warning and take the opportunity without thorough investigation, you will probably end up regretting it. For example, the opportunity could cost you far more money than was initially presented to you. Another example: You accept a promotion not knowing it will require you to sell your house and move to a location you don't like. Never ignore negative warnings—they're there to help you avert trouble.

Key word: Opportunity.

Polarity: Positive.

Literal meaning: Never interpreted literally.

CASKET: A casket (or coffin) is a cardinal sign of death. This will not be your death in a present time reading. If you are doing a past life reading, then the death would be yours. The death will be one that has a profound effect on you. It may be the death of someone to whom you are close. It may be the death of someone you know only casually or don't know at all. The key is that you will feel personally affected or changed by the death.

If the casket is coupled with any symbol of a person, you can sometimes determine who the person is. For example, if coupled with a horse, you would know it will be the death of a friend.

Sometimes you can determine how the death will occur if coupled with a symbol for illness or one portraying an accident such as a crashing airplane.

If the casket is coupled with a positive symbol, it will be a peaceful death. The death could affect you by the loss of a loved one, receiving an inheritance, inspiring you to do something creative, propelling you into action to overcome an injustice, and so forth. In any event, it will not be a death to which you react with a casual "I'm sorry," and then dismiss it.

Key words: Someone's death that will have an effect on you.

Polarity: Negative.

Literal meaning: Never interpreted literally.

CASTLE: You need to do a better job of protecting your own interests in every aspect. Look to the rest of the cup for more indications of where. For example, look for symbols that indicate business, love, health, home, etc.

This is a warning to make sure you lock doors and don't allow strangers into your home. At work, be sure a co-worker isn't taking credit for your work or is perhaps "bad mouthing" you. In your love life, make sure you are holding up your end of obligations and that your partner is not slacking off in his or her obligations.

Key words: Protect your interests.
Polarity: Positive.
Literal meaning: Never interpreted literally.

CAT: A cat indicates treachery. The treachery is directed against you. This treachery is usually not life threatening or physically injurious. If the sign meant physical danger for you, the cat would have to be coupled with some highly negative symbol such as a bat or snake.

The cat symbolizes the sneaky, stab-you-in-the-back treachery. Often the person who is doing you harm is someone you know or pretends to be a friend. The treachery is most often directed to hurt your reputation or to deprive you of some opportunity. For example, you are in line for a promotion and a co-worker does or says something to deliberately hurt your chances for promotion.

The cat (treachery) against you is almost guaranteed to be successful if the cat is alone or is coupled with any negative symbol.

However, if coupled with a positive symbol, the treachery will not be as severe. It takes a very powerful positive symbol to completely overcome the effects of the cat. Such positive symbols are the "angel" and "star." There are a few others also.

Key words: Treachery directed against you.
Polarity: Negative.
Literal meaning: If the cat is coupled with a numeral or a
    letter of the alphabet, interpret the cat literally.

CHAIN: A chain indicates that there will be a linked series of events, none in which you have been involved that will ultimately have a profound effect on your life. The effect on your life will always be beneficial, but it may be sad or unpleasant if the chain is coupled with a negative symbol.

Key words: Chain of events that affect your life.
Polarity: Positive.
Literal meaning: Never interpreted literally.

CHAIR: The interpretation for chair depends on whether the chair is empty or filled.

Filled chair: A new person will enter
    your life during the time indicated.

Empty chair: A current person in your life will leave
    your life during the time indicated. In either case, it
    will be someone important to you, and not just a
    casual acquaintance.

Key words for all: Someone entering (filled chair) or leaving (empty chair) your life.

Polarity for all: Neutral.

Literal meaning for all: Never interpreted literally.

CHURCH BUILDING: You are protected from some unpleasant or harmful situation you may be involved in. This is a very strong influence in the cup and will overcome any negative polarity symbol that might be coupled to it.

If the church building is standing alone, not coupled with anything, it indicates a period of protection in general for you and will mitigate any potentially harmful situation. For example, if you were in an automobile accident, you would not be seriously hurt, or perhaps not hurt at all.

Key words: Great personal protection.

Polarity: Highly positive.

Literal meaning: Not usually interpreted literally, but in rare cases, it could indicate that you might need to take refuge in a church or other sanctified place, so keep this in mind as you interpret the cup. Use your intuitive powers to know when to apply this interpretation.

CHURCH STEEPLE: The church steeple signifies that you will have an enlightening experience which will open up new vistas of knowledge. You will gain greater understanding of self and of what life is about. The outcome will be greater happiness and peace of mind than you have ever known.

This is not a religious experience; it is a spiritual experience. There is a vast difference in the two and you will come to understand that during the time indicated in the cup. What you learn and experience during this period will alter your life forever for the better.

This is an extremely powerful positive symbol that is not often seen in the tea cup, and it never couples with any other symbol regardless of how close they are.

Key words: Enlightening experience.
Polarity: Positive.
Literal meaning: Never interpreted literally.

CIGAR or **CIGARETTE:** The cigar signifies that you will find yourself in the company of good friends. They will be comforting you or wishing you well.

If the cigar is by itself, your friends will be wishing you well because you are moving away or have received a promotion or some recognition.

If the cigar is coupled with a negative symbol, your friends will be comforting you for some sadness or misfortune.

If coupled with a positive symbol, your friends will be helping you celebrate some event such as marriage, birth of a child, winning the lottery, etc.

Key words: In the company of good friends.
Polarity: Positive.
Literal meaning: Never interpreted literally.

CIRCLE OF DOTS: A circle of dots indicates that you will be either taking or planning a vacation during the indicated time. Do not confuse the circle of dots with a solid, or nearly solid, circle or ring which has an entirely different meaning.

If there are any symbols inside the circle of dots, they will pertain to the vacation. Any symbols outside the circle of dots do not pertain to the vacation even though they may be closely placed.

Key word: Vacation.
Polarity: Positive.
Literal meaning: Never interpreted literally.

CLAW: A claw is a symbol of danger. This is physical danger to you. Often this pertains to your work but it is not restricted to that. During the time period indicated, you should exercise good judgment, be aware of what is around you, don't act in haste, and so on.

If the claw is by itself, you will probably be hurt but not seriously. If the claw is coupled with any positive symbol, you will probably have a close call but will escape unharmed.

If the claw is coupled with a negative symbol, you could be seriously hurt. You can avert any harm by being cautious and prudent in your actions. This is not a time to be exceeding the speed limit, taking risks, going swimming alone, etc. Be sensible!

Key word: Danger.
Polarity: Negative.
Literal meaning: Never interpreted literally.

CLOCK: A clock indicates that time is running out for you to take advantage of some opportunity. You have been playing it safe—cautious, no risks. You haven't been sticking your neck out. As a result, your life has been humdrum. You have ideas that you haven't expressed. You have things you would like to try, but haven't.

The clock suggests that now is the time for you to start doing things you only dreamed of before life passes you by. The clock says, "Strike now!" It is not affected by any negative symbols, so you are guaranteed some measure of success, if you act when the clock says to.

Key words: Time to act.
Polarity: Positive.
Literal meaning: Never interpreted literally.

CLOUDS: Clouds are temporary problems that will quickly pass. You will be overly concerned about something that is quite minor and unimportant. Remember, the Sun always comes out after the clouds pass.

Whatever your problems are during the time indicated by the clouds, don't worry. The problems will quickly pass and you will be no worse for the wear.

Key words: Temporary problems.
Polarity: Neutral.
Literal meaning: Never interpreted literally.

CLOVER: This is the premier symbol of good fortune. Whether it is the three-leaf clover or the four-leaf clover, you can be assured of good fortune if this symbol is in your cup.

The difference between the three-leaf and the four-leaf is that the four-leaf clover promises phenomenal good fortune. The three-leaf is great good fortune, but less than the four-leaf symbol.

Even if the clover is coupled with a strong negative symbol, the power of the clover will prevail in the end.

Key words: Good fortune.
Polarity: Highly positive.
Literal meaning: Never interpreted literally.

CLUB: This is the symbol of the kind of club that could be used as a weapon. The kind of club that appears on an ordinary deck of playing cards should be interpreted as a "clover" (see *Clover*).

The weapon club indicates that you will encounter a situation in which someone will attempt to force you to do something against your will. This could be either a situation in which someone uses a form of blackmail against you, or it could be that they will actually force you to do what they want either by threat or by physical force. Whether or not they succeed depends on how intimidated you are by their threat or blackmail.

The kind of situation the club often refers to is this: you cheat on your time card at work by entering time worked when you actually were absent attending to some personal matter. A co-worker knows about it and threatens to tell the supervisor, who would fire you, unless you give something to the co-worker such as a "loan" of a hundred dollars or a sexual favor.

Key words: Attempt to force you to do something against your will.

Polarity: Negative.

Literal meaning: Never interpreted literally.

COBWEB: A cobweb indicates that you will be protected or shielded by someone. Perhaps a co-worker will speak up on your behalf, or perhaps someone will keep you from being harmed in an accident. It could be protection or shielding in most any manner. The shielding or protecting will always be by a person, not by an object.

Key words: Shielded. Protected.

Polarity: Positive.

Literal meaning: Never interpreted literally.

COMB: A comb indicates that you need to improve your personal grooming. The comb is similar to the interpretation for a hairbrush (see *Brush*) except the comb is not as severe a situation as would be indicated by the hairbrush.

The comb means you are sloppy or untidy and need to improve. If left unheeded, your personal grooming could deteriorate to become as serious as that indicated by the hairbrush.

Key words: Need to improve your personal grooming.
Polarity: Negative.
Literal meaning: Never interpreted literally.

COMET: The comet signifies that the time has arrived for you to realize the fulfillment of some goal or dream that you have been anticipating and working for. This is your moment of achievement.

Key words: Your time of fulfillment has arrived.
Polarity: Highly positive.
Literal meaning: Never interpreted literally.

CONDOM: This is a stern warning that your health is in danger. It could be danger from any sort of illness, not just sexual disease. In any case, you would be wise to see your health practitioner for a complete health check-up, including a thorough blood work-up and x-rays.

Key words: Danger to your health.
Polarity: Negative
Literal meaning: Never interpreted literally.

CORN: If a full ear of corn appears in the tea cup, it signifies that you will experience a full, healthy, enjoyable life.

If the corn appears to be only a cob, or only has a few kernels of corn on it, then it indicates that your life will be marred by poor health.

Key words: Full ear—full, healthy life. Unfilled ear—poor health.

Polarity: Full ear—positive. Unfilled ear—negative.
Literal meaning: Never interpreted literally.

COW: The literal interpretation of a cow is multiplication. This means that you will have abundance in your life or work in some manner. It could mean multiple occupations, or many children, or even many marriages.

If the cow is coupled with another symbol, you can often determine to what the multiplication applies.

The cow by itself simply means multiplication in some manner in your life.

Many tea leaf readers interpret the cow to mean many children if you are a woman, and many jobs if you are a man. I try to analyze the cup more thoroughly to see if the cow might not indicate something else. If I don't find something else, then I use the usual interpretation just given.

Key word: Multiplication.
Polarity: Neutral.
Literal meaning: Never interpreted literally.

CRAB: If the crab is alone (not coupled with some other symbol), it indicates that you will be dealing with a cranky, negative, difficult person during the time indicated. This person will be a significant irritant to you.

If the crab is coupled with any symbol that indicates people other than yourself, then it indicates a feast.

Key words: A cranky, difficult person. A feast, if coupled with symbols of people.

Polarity: Neutral.
Literal meaning: Never interpreted literally.

CRADLE: The cradle indicates that a significant substitution will be made in your life during the indicated time period.

A few of the many possible substitutions could be accepting a job you really don't want in place of the one you really wanted; accepting a date or mate that really isn't your first choice; having to cancel your planned vacation because of unplanned events; and so forth.

Key words: Substitution.
Polarity: Negative.
Literal meaning: Never interpreted literally.

CROSS: This is a powerful positive symbol to have in a tea cup. It indicates that you will be able to overcome whatever troubles you are dealing with. It doesn't promise that it will be easy, but you will overcome and triumph if you hang on and keep doing the very best you can to deal with the situation.

No negative symbol in the cup is strong enough to completely overcome the power of the cross in the cup.

Key words: Overcome your troubles.
Polarity: Highly positive.
Literal meaning: Never interpreted literally.

CROSSED BONES: This is one of the classic symbols of a warning. It usually warns you to beware of some person who is out to do you harm. The harm may be to your body, your property, or to your reputation and character.

Most often when I've seen this in the cup of someone for whom I am reading, it has indicated one of two things: a co-worker who is trying to undermine them at work by lying or some other devious means; or a spouse or lover who is cheating on them. Once I saw it coupled to a dollar sign in the cup of a banker's wife. Her husband was stealing from the bank and she lost her home and savings in order to make restitution.

This is not a symbol to take lightly.

Key word: Warning.
Polarity: Highly negative.
Literal meaning: Never interpreted literally.

CROWN: The crown signifies that respect and honor will be given to you, most likely for some achievement.

If the crown is by itself or if it is coupled with some positive symbol, you will be well deserving of the honor.

If the crown is coupled with a negative symbol, you will eventually bring dishonor to yourself through your own lack of integrity, due in part to the fact that you really didn't deserve the honor in the first place.

Key words: Honor. Respect.

Polarity: Positive.

Literal meaning: Never interpreted literally.

CRUTCH: A crutch signifies assistance. If the crutch is coupled with a symbol that indicates another person, then you'll be giving assistance to someone else. Otherwise, the crutch indicates that you will be in need of, and will receive, assistance of some sort from someone.

Key words: Assistance. Help.

Polarity: Positive.

Literal meaning: Never interpreted literally.

CRYSTAL: Crystal signifies clarity of thought and mental vision. You will be able to see every situation you are involved in with crystal-clear understanding. Your mental vision will be clear and uncluttered allowing your creative abilities to be especially powerful and effective.

Key words: Clear thought and vision.

Polarity: Positive.

Literal meaning: Never interpreted literally.

CUP: A cup indicates criticism. There are three different aspects to the criticism, depending on the position of the cup.

Upright cup: If the symbol is upright as you hold the tea cup upright, it indicates that you will receive valid constructive criticism which you will do well to listen to and heed.

Spilling cup: If the cup symbol is tilted to allow the contents to spill out, it indicates that the criticism you receive has some validity but that it is not all valid. You should listen and decide for yourself what is valid. You should be prepared to defend yourself in the face of the invalid criticism.

Overturned cup: The overturned cup indicates that you will receive unjust criticism that is not valid. Do not accept this criticism nor allow it to bother you. The ones doing the criticizing are aware that it is they, not you, who have the problem. Be firm in your rebuking those who give the unjust criticism.

Key word for all: Criticism.
Polarity for all: Neutral.
Literal meaning for all: Never interpreted literally.

-𝒟-

DEER: A deer is a timid person whom you will meet or become involved with in some way. If you make the effort to get to know this timid person, you will gain a valuable, lifelong friend.

Key words: Timid person.
Polarity: Positive.
Literal meaning: Never interpreted literally.

DESK: A desk pertains to your occupation regardless of what your occupation is.

The desk by itself signifies that you feel tied down or restricted by your occupation and you long for a change.

If the desk is coupled with another symbol, then you must blend the symbols to obtain the meaning of the desk. For example, if an antelope is next to the desk, it would indicate that you will be finding new adventure or experience through your occupation. A crown next to the desk indicates that you will receive honors and recognition through your occupation.

Key words: Pertains to your occupation.
Polarity: Neutral.
Literal meaning: Never interpreted literally.

DIAMOND SHAPE: This signifies that you will receive a gift of jewelry during the time period indicated.

Key words: Gift of jewelry.
Polarity: Positive.
Literal meaning: Never interpreted literally.

DICE: You will be taking a chance on something. It could be a chance on a new job, a marriage, the lottery, or even risking your life or health by careless driving, careless nutrition, etc. By itself, dice do not indicate winning or losing, but merely that you are taking a chance.

If coupled with a negative symbol, the outcome will not be to your benefit. If coupled with a positive symbol, the outcome will be to your benefit.

Key words: Taking a chance.

Polarity: Neutral.

Literal meaning: The dice could be taken literally if you are a person who gambles by shooting craps. Otherwise, dice are not interpreted literally.

DINOSAUR: This indicates extreme stubbornness and unwillingness to change. This is a neutral symbol, being neither good nor bad in itself. Stubbornness can bring good or bad into the person's life depending on what the stubbornness is about. If there are any symbols coupled with the dinosaur, you will have a clue as to the outcome.

Stubbornness can cause a person to miss out on opportunities. It can also prevent tragedies. For example, one who stubbornly refuses to take drugs even though all their friends do obviously benefits from being stubborn. If the person stubbornly refuses to improve their work performance, they will not advance in their work, so here it has a negative result.

If the entire cup in general has a good, positive message, then you can interpret the dinosaur as being a beneficial stubbornness. Otherwise, it is a stubbornness that can cause loss of opportunity or even loss of a friendship.

Key words: Extreme stubbornness and unwillingness to change.

Polarity: Neutral.
Literal meaning: Never interpreted literally.

DIRIGIBLE (AIRSHIP): The interpretation for dirigible is "slow moving events." During the period indicated in the cup, time will seem to almost stand still. You will be impatient for things to happen, for results to materialize, for tomorrow to come. But time will drag its feet, and this will cause you much anxiety and frustration.

Most likely it will be a period in which you had expected some action or results, thus heightening your impatience. Be forewarned—you may as well just relax and stop worrying because nothing monumental is going to happen during this period. Things will come when they come, only later.

Key words: Slow-moving events.
Polarity: Neutral.
Literal meaning: Never interpreted literally.

DISH: A dish indicates that you will receive an invitation. It could be any sort of invitation, but usually it is an invitation to dinner or to a night on the town. Almost always, it will be an invitation from someone who has not previously invited you out.

Key words: An invitation.
Polarity: Neutral.
Literal meaning: Never interpreted literally.

DOG: A dog signifies a faithful friend. This isn't just a casual friend or acquaintance, but rather a true, loyal friend who'll be there for you when you need him or her.

If the dog is by itself in the cup, it indicates that your friend will be there to give you companionship and comfort during your troubles.

If the dog is coupled with another symbol you must blend the two symbols to determine the meaning. For example, if a crutch is next to the dog you will need to give aid or assistance to your friend. If a dollar sign is next to the dog, your friend will come into money.

Key words: Faithful friend.

Polarity: Positive.

Literal meaning: If the dog is coupled with a numeral or a letter of the alphabet, interpret the dog literally.

DOLLAR SIGN ($): A dollar sign always indicates money, usually a lot of it.

If this symbol appears all by itself in your cup, it indicates that money will play an important role in your life during the time period concerned.

If the dollar sign is coupled with another symbol, you can obtain the meaning by blending the meanings of the two symbols.

Key word: Money.

Polarity: Positive.

Literal meaning: Always interpreted literally as money.

DOOR: Any sort of door, archway, or entrance indicates opportunity, a new path opening up for you; new possibilities. During the time period indicated, the possibilities will materialize and you will be in a position to take advantage of them.

If the door seems to be closed, it indicates that you currently are not aware of what may lie ahead for you.

If the door is open, it indicates that you are aware of some potential possibilities and are working toward making some things happen for you.

Key words: Opportunity. Possibilities. New paths opening up.

Polarity: Positive.

Literal meaning: Never interpreted literally.

DRAGON: The dragon signifies that you are fooling yourself about something. You have deluded yourself concerning some aspect of your life. During the indicated time period, you will come face to face with your delusion, and you will be forced to face the truth.

If you face the truth with maturity and wisdom, you will emerge a better person.

If you choose to disregard the truth, or to blame someone or something else, you will sink deeper into the fictional world of delusion that you have created for yourself, thus detracting from your self-worth.

Key words: Self-delusion.

Polarity: Negative.
Literal meaning: Never interpreted literally.

-E-

EAR: The symbol of an ear (any kind, human or animal) indicates that you will receive good news during the time period indicated. You could receive it from any source—newspaper, telephone, mail, in person, etc.

If the ear is coupled with another symbol, you can obtain more detail about the news. For example, if coupled with a dog you will receive the good news from a faithful friend. If coupled with a dollar sign, it will be good news about money.

Key words: Good news.
Polarity: Positive.
Literal meaning: Never interpreted literally.

EARRING: An earring indicates that you will sustain a loss of some sort. While it may be a loss of any kind, it most often pertains to a loss of money or property. If the earring is not coupled with another symbol, the loss will be substantial but not devastating.

If coupled with a positive symbol, the loss will be minor and you will recover from it quickly.

Key words: Loss of some kind.
Polarity: Negative.
Literal meaning: Never interpreted literally.

EGG: The interpretation of an egg depends on whether the egg is unbroken or broken.

Unbroken egg: A whole, unbroken egg signifies that your plans and work have been properly executed to ensure your success and that your success will begin to flourish within a very short period. The whole egg is the cardinal sign of new beginnings, a new lifestyle, a new venture, etc.

Broken egg: A broken egg indicates that your plans and work are flawed and will not bring you success. The remedy here is to re-examine your plans and work meticulously, making corrections as needed so that you can turn this potential failure into success.

Keep in mind that symbols in the cup are not fatalistic. You have the power to change many things. This is why tea leaf reading gives you an advantage; it enables you to see the possibilities and then take constructive steps to change those things you can change.

Key words for all: Unbroken egg—success assured based on your solid plans and work. Broken egg—failure assured based on your flawed plans and work.

Polarity for all: Unbroken egg—highly positive. Broken egg—negative.

Literal meaning for all: Never interpreted literally.

EGG BEATER: There will be a mixup in the person's life during the time indicated in the cup. The mixup is rarely serious and almost always turns out to be beneficial in the end. Most often it is a mixup in communication between you and someone else.

If it is coupled with another symbol, you can get an idea what the mixup is about. For example, if coupled with a dollar sign, it would be a mixup over money, such as thinking you had paid a bill when you hadn't.

Only when coupled with the most negative of symbols such as a bat is there need for concern. When coupled with one of the highly negative symbols, the mixup will bring serious problems into the person's life.

Key words: A mixup in your life, usually not serious.
Polarity: Positive.
Literal meaning: Never interpreted literally.

ELEPHANT: The elephant is a powerful positive sign in a cup because it assures long life and endurance.

With this symbol in your cup, you can literally destroy any negative force that assails you. Thus you have phenomenal resistance to illness, and amazing recuperative powers if you should become ill or injured. Of course, you can trample any opposition in your life.

If the elephant is coupled with a negative symbol, you will experience some temporary problems but you will always triumph in the end.

Key words: Long life. Endurance.
Polarity: Highly positive.
Literal meaning: Never interpreted literally.

EYE: The eye always refers to your innate ability to see things through your inner eye; that is, you possess what is commonly referred to as psychic ability.

When you have an eye in your cup, interpret it to mean that you should use more of your higher mind (inner eye) or intuitive intelligence to solve your problems and to find answers. Start listening to that still, small voice within that gives you valid information if you will only listen. Follow your hunches.

Key words: Psychic ability.
Polarity: Positive.
Literal meaning: Never interpreted literally.

EYEGLASSES: Eyeglasses indicate that you need to spend some quiet time by yourself for introspection. You need to re-examine your beliefs, your goals, your philosophy. The reason you need to do this is because you either have strayed away from the course that is best for you, or else you have never really established a course to follow.

Establish goals. Begin to understand who you are, where you are going, and where you really want to go. Have a frank, honest talk with yourself. Use the tea cup to help you find answers and the right direction.

Key word: Introspection.
Polarity: Positive.
Literal meaning: Never interpreted literally.

-F-

FACE: Interpret a face in the cup as being you unless you have the distinct impression that it is some specific person you know.

If it is someone you know, interpret the face as literally representing that person. The meaning of the face depends on the direction it is facing.

Looking backward: If the face is looking back toward the left edge of the cup handle, it signifies that you dwell too much on the past. This results in your missing out on the present and not preparing for the future. The remedy is for you to release the past and start living for NOW with an eye on the future.

Looking forward: If the face is looking forward in time (toward the right edge of the cup handle), it indicates that you can look forward to a life of achievement.

Facing outward: If the face is looking outward toward the interior of the cup, it indicates that you have found the right balance within yourself concerning the past, present, and future. You live in the present to the fullest, learn from the past, and prepare for the future.

Key words for all: Looking backward—dwell too much on the past. Looking forward—a life of achievement. Looking outward—good balance within self.

Polarity for all: Neutral.

Literal meaning for all: The face is always interpreted literally as being a face. The direction that the face is looking determines the exact interpretation.

FAN: This is the hand-held fan, not the electric driven one. This fan indicates pride.

If it is not coupled with another symbol it simply means that you have a great deal of pride in general. If coupled with a desk, for example, it indicates that you take pride in your work. If coupled with a mirror, it indicates pride in who you are as a person, to the point of conceit.

Key word: Pride.

Polarity: Neutral.

Literal meaning: Never interpreted literally.

FEATHER: A feather means instability, insincerity, undependability. If the feather is by itself in the cup, it means that you have these traits.

If it is coupled with other symbols, you must blend the interpretations to obtain the precise meaning. For example, a feather coupled with an anvil or desk indicates that your job is unstable. If coupled with a horse, it means you have a friend who is insincere and unde-pendable. If coupled with a dollar sign, it signifies that your money situation is unstable, and so forth.

Key words: Unstable. Insincere. Undependable.
Polarity: Negative.
Literal meaning: Never interpreted literally.

FENCE: The fence indicates limitations and restrictions in your life in general, if it is not coupled with any other symbol. If coupled with other symbols, it indicates spe-cific limitations or restrictions; for example, a limited number of friends, limited financial resources, limited travel, etc.

In an extreme case, if coupled with a serious negative symbol such as a coiled snake, it could indicate being incarcerated in a jail or hospital or being confined to your home.

Key words: Limitations. Restrictions.
Polarity: Negative.
Literal meaning: Never interpreted literally.

FERRIS WHEEL: The ferris wheel indicates some sort of major distur-bance in your life during the time period specified in the tea cup.

If it is coupled with some other symbol, you can get a more specific clue as to what sort of disturbance. For example, if coupled with a crashing airplane, it would indicate that an accident during travel (by any mode, not just air) would cause a major disturbance in your life.

If coupled with a four-leaf clover, some major stroke of good fortune would turn your life upside down.

Key word: Disturbance.

Polarity: Negative.

Literal meaning: Never interpreted literally.

FINGER: A finger forewarns you of a problem that is headed your way. Usually the problem will not occur within the same time period that the finger appears. The warning is usually one to three months in advance.

The nature of the pending problem will not be apparent unless the finger is coupled with some symbol that sheds some light on it. For example, if the finger is coupled to a desk, you might expect to be laid off from your job. If you have some inkling of what might be coming, you can start preparing yourself for it.

Key word: Forewarned.

Polarity: Negative.

Literal meaning: Never interpreted literally.

FIRE: Fire is emotion—anger, lust, passion, hatred, love, elation, ecstasy. Where fire appears in your cup, you will have a very emotional experience, an experience that will penetrate the depths of your soul. Whether it is a beneficial or detrimental experience depends on how it is coupled with other symbols.

Fire by itself just indicates a deeply emotional experience. Since you know the experience is coming you can start working now on your self-control so that whatever happens it doesn't get out of hand and become an unpleasant experience.

Key word: Emotion.
Polarity: Negative.
Literal meaning: If the fire is coupled with a numeral or a letter of the alphabet, interpret the fire literally.

FIRECRACKER: The firecracker signifies excitement. The usual implication is that the excitement is enjoyable.

If the firecracker is coupled with a negative symbol, then the excitement would be unpleasant. Look to any coupled symbol for more detail.

Key word: Excitement.
Polarity: Positive.
Literal meaning: Never interpreted literally.

FIREPLACE: A fireplace is always a positive symbol, and it means comfort, security, well-being, peace of mind.

When coupled with a negative symbol, the fireplace prevents the implications of the negative symbol from having any serious effect on you. For example, suppose the fireplace is coupled with a bat. You would never be harmed by the treachery posed by the bat. The treachery would be there, but it would never get off the ground, so to speak. You would be protected.

Key words: Comfort. Security. Well-being. Peace of
mind.
Polarity: Highly positive.
Literal meaning: Never interpreted literally.

FISH: With one exception, the shark,
any fish in the tea cup is a positive
symbol that indicates an increase in
either your material wealth or your
spiritual growth.

If the fish is not coupled with another symbol, the
interpretation is material gain.

If coupled with a spiritual sign, such as a cross, it
indicates spiritual growth. If coupled with a horse, it
indicates material gain through a friend.

If there are many fish, then there will be a great deal of
gain. However, if the fish is definitely a shark, you need
to beware because someone is out to take away some of
your possessions, either through theft, deceit, or trickery.
If a shark is in your cup, take time to thoroughly read
and understand everything you sign during the time period indicated. During this period, salespeople will be truly
cunning in trying to part you from your money.

Key words: Increase in material wealth or spiritual
growth. If a shark, loss of material wealth.
Polarity: In general—positive. If a shark—negative.
Literal meaning: If the fish is coupled with a numeral or
a letter of the alphabet, interpret the fish literally.

FISHING POLE: The fishing pole indicates that you will be involved in some sort of investigation. This does not necessarily imply that it is a legal or criminal investigation, although it could be if the pole is coupled with other symbols which might indicate that.

The fishing pole by itself could mean anything from investigating the housing market in order to make the best purchase to investigating someone's background in conjunction with an employment application.

If the fishing pole has a fishing line on it, then you will be involved in actually doing the investigation in some way. If the fishing pole does not have a line on it, then you will be the one who is investigated.

As with most symbols, you can obtain more information if the pole is coupled with other symbols.

Key word: Investigation.
Polarity: Neutral.
Literal meaning: Never interpreted literally.

FIST: A fist indicates that it is time for you to become tenacious—to hold on tightly. Don't give up, regardless of the opposition or odds. If you "hang tough," you will succeed over whatever obstacles are presented to you.

This fist applies to any aspect of your life. If you are in a race for elective office, and you have a fist in your cup, all you need to do to win is to hang on and not buckle under the pressure. The fist tells you to fight, not with violence, but with spirit.

Key words: Tenacity. Hang tough. Don't give up.
Polarity: Positive.
Literal meaning: Never interpreted literally.

FLAG ON A POLE: A flag on a pole
tells you that it is imperative you maintain the highest standards and integrity
in order to achieve your goals.

This symbol will appear during the time period when
you will be greatly tempted to compromise your ideals,
beliefs, or standards in order to either please someone
else or to quickly gain some immediate advantage. This
symbol warns that if you give into this sort of compromise you will pay dearly in the long run. The short-term
gain will not be worth the long-term loss.

Pay close attention to this symbol because it indicates
a turning point in your life for better or worse, depending on the choices you make at that time.

Key words: Maintain integrity. Turning point in life.
Don't compromise your standards.
Polarity: Neutral.
Literal meaning: Never interpreted literally.

FLASHLIGHT: This indicates that you have been
focusing your life and abilities in too narrow a scope.
You have considerably more ability than you have begun
to use. You have been depriving yourself of fulfillment
and enrichment because you have not allowed yourself
to accept a broader range of experiences and learning.

What you need to do is deliberately branch out and embrace new avenues of experience. Perhaps you need to travel, take vacations, take up a hobby, get a more challenging job, do volunteer work, or something else.

You will need to analyze your situation to see what might be the direction for you to embark on.

Mostly, you need an attitude change. Start thinking "I can" and stop thinking "I can't." Start doing instead of thinking about doing. Start thinking "I will" instead of "I'll try."

Key words: Focus of life too narrow. Limiting attitude.
Polarity: Negative.
Literal meaning: Never interpreted literally.

FLOWER: Flowers indicate that you will receive compliments during the time period indicated. These are not likely to be profound compliments, but they will be sufficient to impress you and stick in your mind.

One flower is a more powerful symbol than many flowers because one indicates that you will receive a sincere compliment from a person that will mean a great deal to you. Often it will be a compliment from someone who never gives compliments, or it may be one from an expert or authority figure from whom such a compliment carries a great deal of weight and importance.

Occasionally, it will even be a compliment from an avowed adversary; these are the most meaningful of all compliments.

Key word: Compliments.

Polarity: Positive.

Literal meaning: If the flowers are coupled with a numeral or a letter of the alphabet, interpret the flowers as being flowers.

FLY: A fly signifies illness, usually one connected with unsanitary conditions. During the period of time when the fly appears in the cup, you should exercise extra precautions about your health. Wash fruits and vegetables before eating them. Cook food thoroughly. Keep your hands clean and your fingers out of your mouth. Don't eat off others' plates or drink out of unwashed glasses, and so forth.

If the fly is coupled with a positive symbol, your illness will be slight, more of an inconvenience than anything else.

If the fly is by itself, your illness could go either way, depending on the care you give yourself.

If the fly is coupled with a negative symbol, you will likely get sick enough to have to stay in bed for a day or two. The fly would have to be coupled with two or more negative symbols before the illness would be serious enough to be life threatening.

Key word: Illness.

Polarity: Negative.

Literal meaning: Never interpreted literally.

FOOT: A foot indicates that you will be entering, or stepping into, a new experience during the time period indicated. This will be a significant new experience, not something ordinary. For instance, it would be a new profession, a new love, an exciting trip, a psychic or spiritual experience, and so forth.

If the foot also has a leg attached, it will be a profound experience that will affect you for the rest of your life. Whatever the experience, it will be a major event or turning point in your life in some way.

Key words: Stepping into a new experience.
Polarity: Positive.
Literal meaning: If the foot is coupled to a numeral or a
    letter of the alphabet, interpret the foot literally.

FOOTBALL: The football indicates that you will be involved in a political situation in your work in which you find yourself caught between two opposing powers.

You need to be careful because each of these two opposing powers is likely to use you for their own gain. They are manipulators, and you could well be an innocent person who will be manipulated.

Watch for the signs of a power struggle in your work and then go to great lengths to stay out of it. If you do so, you will be fine.

If you get involved or take sides, you will be the one who ends up on the short end of things. In essence, you are likely to be a pawn in a chess game of manipulation. Pawns are the pieces that get sacrificed.

If the football is coupled with a negative symbol, you need to be extremely careful because you could end up being blamed for something you are not guilty of. In other words, you could become a scapegoat.

Key words: Political pawn. Scapegoat.
Polarity: Negative.
Literal meaning: Never interpreted literally.

FOREST: A forest signifies that your thinking has become muddled and unclear. As a result, you don't recognize truth or reality. In extreme cases, if the forest is coupled with a strong negative symbol such as a coiled snake, your mental health could be at stake.

The most common situation is that you will do or say things which will drive friends and loved ones away from you if you refuse to accept the fact that it is your thinking, not theirs, that is at fault.

Almost always, this mental situation is brought on by your inability to handle stress in a healthy manner. Since you know this situation is ahead of you, take steps now to learn how to manage stress. Then you will avert or lessen the problem.

Key words: Muddled, unclear thinking.
Polarity: Negative.
Literal meaning: Never interpreted literally.

FORK: A fork in your tea cup means that you will be assisted at the moment when you most need it.

The fork does not indicate why you will need assistance, only that you will receive it. Other symbols in the cup may give a clue as to why you might need help.

Key words: Receiving assistance.
Polarity: Positive.
Literal meaning: Never interpreted literally.

FOX: If the fox is not coupled with any other symbol, it indicates that the person's basic nature is one of shrewdness and resourcefulness. The fox is considered to be a strong symbol for good fortune, in general, for business enterprises.

If coupled with a positive symbol, it indicates that shrewdness and resourcefulness will definitely bring success in whatever venture the person is engaged in at the time indicated in the cup.

If coupled with a negative symbol, it indicates there will be a need for shrewdness and resourcefulness in order to prevent problems at the time indicated in the cup.

Key words: Shrewdness and resourcefulness, especially in business.
Polarity: Positive.
Literal meaning: Never interpreted literally.

FROG: If you want to succeed, you must learn to adapt to all situations. If you are a person who doesn't like change or even rebels at change, the frog is telling you that you are limiting your future by such thinking and that to succeed you must embrace change. You must learn to be flexible in your behavior and thinking processes.

The frog is not influenced by nearby negative or positive symbols in the cup. The frog just tells you the way it is if you want to succeed.

Key words: Learn to adapt, to embrace change.
Polarity: Neutral.
Literal meaning: Never interpreted literally.

FRYING PAN: A frying pan indicates that you will be in trouble. It will be a situation in which you will be questioned harshly and at length concerning what you have been doing and what you know. It will not be pleasant. Even if you are innocent of any wrongdoing, you will be treated as though you had done something wrong.

If you are guilty of some wrongdoing, the frying pan assures that it will be found out, and you will have to "pay the piper."

If you are innocent, that will be established also. However, there will always be a few people who will believe the worst of you even though you are innocent. You will be subject to the "where there is smoke there is fire" mentality.

Key words: Trouble. Accusations.
Polarity: Negative.
Literal meaning: Never interpreted literally.

FUNNEL: The funnel indicates that you will have many things to accomplish within tight time limits, but no matter how hard you work you will only achieve a limited amount of progress.

The problem is that you expect too much of yourself and of others, that your planning is haphazard instead of being organized, and that you do not work efficiently.

This will be a period of frustration that will give you the opportunity to learn patience, to learn how to work smarter rather than just harder, and to become more philosophical in your approach to life in general. If you learn the lessons, you will suddenly find progress and peace of mind. If not, you will have future opportunities to repeat the frustrations until you decide to learn.

Key words: Period of frustration. Lessons to be learned.
Polarity: Neutral.
Literal meaning: Never interpreted literally.

-*G*-

GALLOWS: A gallows in the tea cup indicates trouble. If the gallows is coupled with a negative symbol, it will be serious trouble that will cause disruption in your life, probably cost you a considerable amount of money, and will be with you for a long time.

If coupled with a positive symbol, the trouble will be a temporary annoyance with no permanent consequences.

If the gallows is by itself, the trouble will be something that you bring on yourself by your own words and actions or that will cost you the loss of a friendship.

Key word: Trouble.
Polarity: Negative.
Literal meaning: Never interpreted literally.

GAVEL: A gavel indicates that you will be involved with the law and the system of justice. If the gavel is by itself, you will be a witness or will give a deposition in some legal proceedings.

If the gavel is coupled with any positive symbol, you will have to appear in court but will be found not guilty (if a criminal matter) or not at fault (if a civil matter).

If the gavel is coupled with any negative symbol, you will have to appear in court and will be found guilty (if a criminal matter) or at fault (if a civil matter).

Key words: Involvement with the law and justice system.
Polarity: Neutral.
Literal meaning: Never interpreted literally.

GIRAFFE: Interpret this symbol as "taking a chance." If coupled with a positive symbol, this would be a beneficial time to take a chance because the result will likely be exceptionally beneficial.

If by itself, taking a chance will be beneficial, but not as beneficial as when coupled with a positive symbol.

If coupled with a negative symbol, taking chances at this time would prove detrimental, so do not take chances during the time period indicated in the cup.

Key words: Taking a chance.
Polarity: Positive.
Literal meaning: Never interpreted literally.

GLASS, DRINKING: This symbol signifies that you thirst for more fulfillment in life.

The glass by itself merely indicates your dissatisfaction with your life as it is now, but it does not offer any solutions for you.

If coupled with other symbols it will either identify exactly what your dissatisfaction is or will suggest possible courses of action for you. For example, if coupled with a heart shape, it indicates that you wish to have a meaningful love or relationship in your life. If coupled with an airplane, it suggests that travel will offer a solution for you, even if only a temporary one.

Key words: Dissatisfaction with life.
Polarity: Neutral.
Literal meaning: Never interpreted literally.

GLASS, WINE (COCKTAIL GLASS, etc.): A wine glass signifies that you will be attending a celebration of some sort during the time period indicated. If the wine glass is by itself, you will be celebrating something personal such as your birthday, wedding, anniversary, etc.

If the wine glass is coupled with any positive symbol, you will be attending someone else's personal celebration.

If the wine glass is coupled with any negative symbol, you will be attending some sort of public or social celebration. For example, a centennial celebration for the state in which you reside.

Key word: Celebration.
Polarity: Positive.
Literal meaning: Never interpreted literally.

GOAT: The goat symbolizes stubborn determination to win when faced with opposition. You cannot push a goat because the goat always pushes back. In the tea cup, this means that you will be faced with a difficult situation in which you must act and react as a goat if you want to triumph; that is, you must have stubborn determination.

You must fight back. You must take an active, aggressive role on your own behalf. If you do not act as a goat in this situation, you will not win.

The opposite of goat is sheep (see *Sheep*). In difficult situations there are times when it is best to act as a goat. Other times it is best to act as a sheep. Let the tea cup be your guide.

Key words: Stubborn determination. Aggressive. Active.
Polarity: Positive.
Literal meaning: Never interpreted literally.

GRAPES, BUNCH OF: A bunch of grapes indicates abundant health for you. If the grapes are coupled with a symbol that indicates another person, it means abundant health for that person.

If the grapes are coupled with any symbol other than one for another person, do not interpret the symbols as being coupled; interpret them separately.

Key words: Abundant health.
Polarity: Positive.
Literal meaning: Never interpreted literally.

GRASS: Grass indicates that you will have all that you will need in the way of material possessions and security. Grass is one of the symbols that, like grapes, can be coupled only with the symbol for another person.

With another person, grass indicates that that person will have all the material possessions and security they need. Other symbols should be interpreted separately.

Key words: Sufficient material wealth.
Polarity: Positive.
Literal meaning: Never interpreted literally as grass.

GUN: A gun symbolizes anger. A gun is a neutral symbol, neither positive nor negative. It is how it is used that determines whether it is positive or negative. The same as with anger.

Violent anger that causes you to strike out at an innocent person is a negative anger. An anger against injustice that causes you to crusade for justice is a positive anger.

A gun in your cup indicates that you will be angry about some situation at that time. A handgun signifies a short-lived anger that flares up quickly and then subsides quickly. A rifle indicates an anger that lasts a long time. A cannon or other large gun indicates a deeply ingrained anger that is likely to be with you most of the time all your life.

If the gun is coupled with any symbol which indicates another person, that person will be angry with you.

A gun coupled with a symbol other than another person gives more specific meaning to the anger. For example, coupled with a star indicates that your anger will be publicly displayed; coupled with a desk means that your anger will be directed toward your work environment.

Anger does not become negative by being coupled to a negative symbol, nor does it become positive by being coupled to a positive symbol. Anger is just anger—neutral.

Only you, through your own individual choice and actions, make the anger either positive or negative. When you see a gun in your cup, you alone are responsible for what happens.

Key words: Anger. Personal responsibility for your actions.
Polarity: Neutral.
Literal meaning: If the gun is coupled with a numeral or
   a letter of the alphabet, interpret the gun literally.

-ℋ-

HAIRPIN: The hairpin is a symbol of gossip. If coupled with a negative symbol the gossip will be malicious.

If coupled with a positive symbol, the gossip will be merely "catty." If the hairpin is by itself, the gossip will be harmless, random gossip, not specially directed toward anyone.

In all cases, you will be one of the participants in doing the gossiping. If the hairpin is coupled to a symbol of some person (a horse, dog, etc.) you will be gossiping about that person.

Key words: You will be gossiping.
Polarity: Negative.
Literal meaning: Never interpreted literally.

HAMMER: This symbol indicates that you will be dealing with, and be annoyed by, a complaining person during the time indicated. This person will be a pest.

If the hammer is coupled with any negative symbol, the complaining will have a negative effect on you and you will also become a complainer.

If coupled with any positive symbol, you will do your best to get the complainer to stop and to see the brighter side of life. If the hammer is by itself, you will listen and suffer in silence.

Key words: Subjected to a pesky, complaining person.
Polarity: Negative.
Literal meaning: Never interpreted literally.

HAMMOCK: A hammock in your cup indicates that you will be taking a vacation during the indicated time.

If coupled with a negative symbol, it will not be a completely enjoyable vacation. If the hammock is by itself or coupled with a positive symbol, it will be a thoroughly enjoyable vacation.

Key words: Taking a vacation.
Polarity: Positive.
Literal meaning: Never interpreted literally.

HAND: A hand indicates friendly assistance. If coupled with any symbol indicating another person, you will receive assistance from that person. Otherwise, you will be the one giving the assistance to someone else.

If the hand is coupled with another symbol, you will get a clearer picture of what your assistance will be all about. For example, if coupled with a desk, you will assist someone at work. If coupled with a star, you will give assistance in some situation that will cause the public to notice you.

Key word: Assistance.
Polarity: Positive.
Literal meaning: Never interpreted literally.

HARP: The harp is a highly positive symbol indicating great joy. This can also be a sign of spiritual awareness if coupled with another positive symbol. Wherever a harp appears in your cup, you will experience some of the greatest happiness in your life to date.

Negative symbols have no effect on the harp.

Key words: Great happiness.
Polarity: Highly positive.
Literal meaning: Never interpreted literally.

HAT: A hat of any kind indicates that you will be assuming a new or different role or responsibility. Commonly, it could mean a change of jobs, a promotion, or added responsibilities at work.

It could mean hundreds of other roles also. For example, you become a husband or wife or parent, you are elected president of the PTA or to any other office, you become a juror, and so forth. The hat implies it will be a role of some responsibility.

If the hat is alone or is coupled with a positive symbol, you will perform the new responsibility satisfactorily.

If coupled with a negative symbol, you will not perform as well as expected.

Key words: A new or different role.
Polarity: Positive.
Literal meaning: Never interpreted literally.

HAYSTACK: A haystack in your tea cup literally means "you will now reap what you have sown." In other words, you will gain the rewards of your hard work. Of course, if you have been lazy or dishonest, you will gain the penalties of such behavior.

A haystack, therefore, is neither positive nor negative. It is merely a signifier that predicts when your payday will occur. Your own performance, whether good or bad, determines what kind of payday it will be. The haystack promises karma.

Key words: Karma. You reap what you have sown.
Polarity: Neutral.
Literal meaning: Never interpreted literally.

HEADSTONE (GRAVE): A headstone or a grave indicates that someone's death, usually a recent one, has greatly affected you. You haven't completely gotten over it, probably because there was something unfinished between you and the deceased person. Most likely the deceased person wants to make contact with you one last time to make everything complete and right.

This symbol is not affected by other symbols in the cup even though they may be very closely positioned.

Interpret this symbol by itself as though it is alone in the cup because it has a special message for you. How you handle this situation is dependent on your own beliefs.

Key words: Troubled over a death. Message from beyond the grave.
Polarity: Positive.
Literal meaning: Never interpreted literally.

HEART SHAPE: The heart shape always signifies love, affection, and caring. It can mean you will fall in love or find your true love at the time indicated.

This is a strong, positive symbol that affects and overpowers whatever other symbols it may be coupled with.

Key words: Love. Affection. Caring.
Polarity: Highly positive.
Literal meaning: Never interpreted literally.

Half a Heart Shape: A half of a heart shape in a tea cup indicates an unrequited love; love unreturned. The person (whose cup it is) either loves someone who doesn't return that love or the person doesn't return the love that someone is offering them.

If the half-heart is coupled with any negative symbol, then the unreturned love situation will end bitterly or with bad feelings that are not likely to ever change.

If the half-heart is coupled with any positive symbol or with a neutral polarity symbol, the unreturned love situation will end without any problems or lasting effects.

The half-heart symbol, being neutral, does not have any effect on any other symbol.

Key words: Unrequited love.
Polarity: Neutral.
Literal meaning: Never interpreted literally.

HIGHCHAIR, BABY'S: This signifies a childish, immature person in your life who causes you concern. It could be an employee whose childish behavior causes problems at your workplace. It could be some member of your family or a friend who needs to grow up and accept their responsibilities. You will be the one who will have to counsel this person.

If the highchair is coupled with a positive symbol, your counseling will be successful.

If the highchair is alone, your counseling will be somewhat successful.

If coupled with a negative symbol, your counseling will fall on deaf ears and be unsuccessful.

Key words: You will counsel a childish, immature person.
Polarity: Positive.
Literal meaning: Never interpreted literally.

HILLS: Hills in a tea cup signify spiritual growth. You are becoming more aware; your consciousness is expanding. Truth is becoming the cornerstone of your beliefs and philosophy. You are beginning to understand that you create your own reality.

The appearance of hills in your cup marks a major turning point in your life. The further you ascend the hills of spiritual growth, the further you can see into truth. The further you see into truth, the more complete your life will become.

Key words: Spiritual growth. Truth.
Polarity: Highly positive.

Literal meaning: If coupled with a numeral or a letter of the alphabet, interpret the hills literally.

HOE: The hoe is the symbol of ambitious desire. During the time period the hoe appears in the cup, you will feel an intense desire to succeed, to achieve, to be recognized, to get ahead.

If the hoe is coupled with any positive symbol, you will definitely do something constructive with your ambitious desires. You will get off your duff and work to make your dreams materialize.

If coupled with a negative symbol, you won't do anything except think about getting ahead. The ambition will soon pass, and you will have accomplished nothing.

If the hoe is by itself, you will make some half-hearted attempts to achieve, but will not follow through sufficiently to make much gain. The hoe gives the desire but not the drive to bring the desire to fruition.

Key words: Ambitious desire.
Polarity: Positive.
Literal meaning: Never interpreted literally.

HOLSTER: This indicates that you will not be in any physical danger during the time in which the holster appears.

This does not mean you are protected. It simply means you won't be in any situation in which you need protection. It will be a worry-free, low-key time for you to relax.

Key words: Free from danger.
Polarity: Positive.
Literal meaning: Never interpreted literally.

HOOK: Any sort of hook means that you will be exceptionally inquisitive during this period.

If the hook is by itself or coupled to any positive symbol, your inquisitiveness will be directed toward healthy, constructive learning. You will want to find answers to various philosophical and technical questions. You will be eager to study and explore, always asking Why? How? When? Where? Who? with the intention of increasing your knowledge.

If the hook is coupled with any negative symbol, your inquisitiveness will be plain "nosiness." You will be seeking to intrude into the personal affairs of others for no good reason—just to be nosy and perhaps to gather news for gossip.

Key word: Inquisitiveness.
Polarity: Positive.
Literal meaning: Never interpreted literally.

HORN: The horn refers to self-appreciation. If the horn is by itself, you have a good, balanced feeling of self-worth without being egotistical or overly humble.

If the horn is coupled with any negative symbol, you have an unrealistic view of your worth and importance in the world. You are probably a braggart.

If the horn is coupled with any positive symbol, you are content to do good, honest work and let it speak on your behalf. Others will "toot your horn" for you.

Key words: Self-appreciation.
Polarity: Positive.
Literal meaning: Never interpreted literally.

HORSE: A horse is one of the symbols that stands for someone other than yourself. In this case, it indicates a friend. If the horse is by itself, it indicates simply that you will be involved in activities with a friend during the indicated time period.

If the horse is coupled with any symbol, then you have to interpret the two symbols together to get the meaning. For example, a horse coupled with a fly indicates that you will have a friend who becomes ill. (See *Fly* for the details of the illness.)

Key words: A friend.
Polarity: Positive.
Literal meaning: If the horse is coupled with a numeral or a letter of the alphabet, interpret the horse literally.

HORSESHOE: The horseshoe is always a symbol of good luck. Other symbols near the horseshoe have no effect on it. The horseshoe guarantees good fortune during the time period indicated.

Key words: Good luck.

Polarity: Highly positive.

Literal meaning: Never interpreted literally.

HOUSE: One of the few symbols that is always interpreted literally. It always means house or home.

Key words: House. Home.

Polarity: Neutral.

Literal meaning: Always interpreted as being a house regardless of whether it is alone or coupled.

HURDLES: Hurdles represent obstacles in your path. They are something to be overcome if you are to succeed. If the hurdle is alone in the cup, it is a significant problem or obstacle that you must deal with. You will have the ability to overcome the obstacle, but it won't be easy.

If the hurdle is coupled with any positive symbol, you will conquer the problem quite easily.

If the hurdle is coupled with any negative symbol, the problem will be so significant that you may not be able to overcome it. If you do overcome the problem, it will take such tremendous effort and resources that it may not be really worth it. You could find yourself financially and physically exhausted.

Key word: Obstacles.

Polarity: Negative.

Literal meaning: Never interpreted literally.

-I-

IRON, CLOTHES: A clothes iron means that you have problems that must be resolved (ironed out) now. These problems must not be ignored or postponed because they will be detrimental to your future if you don't deal with them effectively now.

The time indicated in the cup is your best time to handle the problems. This symbol does not give you much time to act. You generally must act within a couple weeks or it will be too late to prevent more serious problems from arising.

Key words: Problems to be resolved.
Polarity: Negative.
Literal meaning: Never interpreted literally.

-J-

JAR: A jar indicates that you will need to borrow something during the time period indicated. Usually it is money, but it could be something else such as a car.

The reason you will need to borrow is poor planning or unwise actions on your part. You overspent. You neglected to get your car repaired when it first showed signs of trouble. You gambled, and so forth.

To prevent the promise of the jar from becoming reality, you should develop better habits now; otherwise you will be caught in a pinch.

Key words: Need to borrow.
Polarity: Negative.
Literal meaning: Never interpreted literally.

JUG: A jug means party time. During the time period in which the jug appears you will be having a good time. It could be a celebration. It could be just a good time in general—nothing special. You will enjoy the company of others. It will be a lighthearted, carefree time for you.

Key words: Party time.
Polarity: Positive.
Literal meaning: Never interpreted literally.

-*K*-

KANGAROO: Indicates instability in the person's life. The person needs to settle down and establish a constructive plan for their life. This symbol does not couple with any other symbol.

Key words: Instability in the person's life.
Polarity: Neutral.
Literal meaning: Never interpreted literally.

KEG: A keg signifies that during the time period indicated in the tea cup you will be storing supplies.

If the keg is by itself or coupled with any positive symbol, you will be finding many excellent buys on merchandise, which you will purchase in large quantities for future use. For example, the local grocer is running a "two for the price of one" sale, so you stock up enough to last through the winter. Or if there is some big-ticket item (TV, refrigerator, car, etc.) that you need, this would be a good time to shop for it because you are certain to find a good buy.

If the key is coupled with any negative symbol, it indicates that you will be storing supplies for some emergency or critical situation. For example, stocking up on a supply of bottled water and canned goods to see you through a hurricane, flood, blizzard, etc.

Key words: Storing supplies.
Polarity: Positive.
Literal meaning: Never interpreted literally.

KETTLE: The kettle means that you will be entertaining house guests during the time period indicated. Almost always it will  be overnight guests, but it can also mean guests for a day visit that will include refreshments and a meal.

If the kettle is by itself or coupled with any positive symbol, the guests will be ones that you welcome and enjoy even if they popped in unexpectedly.

If the kettle is coupled with any negative symbol, the guests will be ones that you really don't enjoy and wish had not come. Usually these will be uninvited guests. However, it also includes guests you invited because you felt obligated even though you really don't care for their company. For example, a relative or in-law who is not one of your favorite people.

Key words: House guests.
Polarity: Neutral.
Literal meaning: Never interpreted literally.

KEY: A key is success. You will achieve some measure of success in some endeavor during the indicated time period. However, the key also prophesies your long-term success in general beyond the time period limitations of the tea cup. The key is not affected one way or the other by any nearby symbols.

Key word: Success.
Polarity: Positive.
Literal meaning: Never interpreted literally.

KITE: A kite indicates that you have set high goals for yourself. If the kite is by itself, the goals are well within your reach and you can achieve them if you are willing to expend hard work and be patient.

If the kite is coupled with any positive symbol, the goals are well within your reach and you will achieve them with minimal effort.

If the kite is coupled with any negative symbol, you have set goals that are unrealistic. You are setting yourself up for possible failure. You would be well advised to re-evaluate yourself and your goals.

Key words: High goals.

Polarity: Positive.

Literal meaning: Never interpreted literally.

KNIFE: A knife signifies fear. During the time indicated in the tea cup, you will experience great fear.

If the knife is by itself, your fear is justified and you should exercise proper precautions. For example, if you fear you have a health problem, see your medical practitioner without delay. If you fear physical harm from someone, alert the police and take whatever steps you deem appropriate to protect yourself.

If the knife is coupled with any positive symbol, your fear is groundless and you should dismiss it.

If the knife is coupled with any negative symbol, your fear is psychosomatic and you should seek professional help because the fear can cause you both mental and physical problems.

Key word: Fear.

Polarity: Negative.

Literal meaning: If the knife is coupled with a numeral or a letter of the alphabet, interpret the knife literally.

KNIGHT: There are two kinds of knights, each with a distinct meaning: a knight such as in King Arthur's Knights of the Round Table, and a chess piece.

Knight (King Arthur's): This signifies obedience. It indicates that you need to exhibit more obedience to a set of values because you have been living a wishy-washy, lackadaisical life.

If you want a life of achievement and value, you must become obedient to some philosophy now; otherwise, you will continue to drift aimlessly.

Knight (Chess Piece): This knight means honor. When this appears in your tea cup, it indicates that you are destined for honor at some time in your life.

Neither kind of knight is affected by nearby symbols.

Key words for all: King Arthur's knight—obedience. Chess piece knight—honor.
Polarity for all: Positive (for both knights).
Literal meaning for all: Never interpreted literally.

KNITTING NEEDLE: The knitting needle indicates effort. Its appearance in your tea cup means that you need to exert more effort in your life, both in playing and in working.

If you want to get something from living, you have to give first. That is what the knitting needle is telling you to do—to start giving with increased effort. The knitting needle is not affected by other nearby symbols.

Key word: Effort.

Polarity: Positive.
Literal meaning: Never interpreted literally.

-⅃-

LADDER: The ladder signifies climbing toward success. During the time period indicated, you will have the opportunity to make some significant strides up the ladder of success if the ladder is by itself.

If the ladder is coupled with any positive symbol, your ultimate success is assured.

If the ladder is coupled with any negative symbol, your climb toward success will be quite difficult with many setbacks. However, you will still succeed if you don't give up.

Key words: Climbing toward success.
Polarity: Positive.
Literal meaning: Never interpreted literally.

LADLE: The ladle simply means that you will be the one who must give some news to someone during the time period indicated.

If the ladle is by itself in the tea cup, you will be giving generic news such as a status report at work, a presentation to a group of people, a business meeting, a fraternal meeting, etc.

If coupled with a positive symbol, you will be delivering good news, usually to one person. For example, informing an employee of a promotion or salary increase.

If the ladle is coupled with any negative symbol, you will be delivering unpleasant news, usually to one person. For example, the person is fired or laid off, or there is a death in the family, etc.

Key words: Delivering news.
Polarity: Neutral.
Literal meaning: Never interpreted literally.

LAMB: The lamb stands for gentleness. In a tea cup, it means that you will be involved in a situation that calls for you to act with gentleness, kindness, and consideration in order to resolve the situation in the best possible manner.

The implication is that if you pass up the opportunity to act with gentleness, you will cause emotional distress to someone and will lose some measure of self-respect for yourself.

Other symbols do not have any effect on the lamb, even if they are located close by.

Be sure you interpret the symbol correctly as being a lamb. A sheep can look very similar to a lamb, but the sheep has a slightly different meaning. (See *Sheep.*) If the symbol is small and lean with no tail, it is a lamb (usually). If it is a little fat, mature looking, and has a tail, it is a sheep (usually).

Key words: Gentleness. Kindness. Consideration.
Polarity: Positive.
Literal meaning: Never interpreted literally.

LAMP: A lamp signifies guidance. You will be in the dark concerning something that you consider significant. Then, just as suddenly as a lamp illuminates a dark room, you will see the light during the time indicated in the tea cup.

If the lamp is by itself in the cup, you will receive the guidance you need through another person.

If the lamp is coupled with any positive symbol, you will receive the guidance through some positive, probably enjoyable, experience or occurrence.

If the lamp is coupled with any negative symbol, you will receive the guidance through some negative, probably unpleasant experience or occurrence.

In any case, you will receive guidance concerning the situation that currently has you in the dark.

Key word: Guidance.
Polarity: Positive.
Literal meaning: Never interpreted literally.

LANTERN: The lantern is the symbol of the pioneer. You will find yourself pioneering some cause or pursuit. For example, you could be trying to get your employer to offer better benefits to the employees; or you may organize a march on the state capitol to protest high taxes.

If the lantern is by itself, you will be doing your pioneering by yourself, without support from others.

If the lantern is coupled with any positive symbol, you will receive support from others.

If coupled with any negative symbol, you will receive serious opposition to your pioneering efforts.

Key word: Pioneering.
Polarity: Positive.
Literal meaning: Never interpreted literally.

LARIAT: The lariat indicates unsuccessful plans. The plans you make during the time period indicated in the tea cup will not materialize. Knowing this in advance, you should either make your plans before the time period or else postpone the plans until after the time period. This way you will avoid disappointment and frustration.

The polarities of nearby symbols have no influence on the lariat.

Key words: Unsuccessful plans.
Polarity: Negative.
Literal meaning: Never interpreted literally.

LEAF: The leaf pertains to your health. If the leaf is by itself, your health will remain just as it is when you enter the indicated time period; that is, your health will be stable, getting neither better nor worse.

If the leaf is coupled to any positive symbol, your health will become stronger, more robust, and energetic.

If coupled to any negative symbol, your health will become poorer in some way. Don't ignore this. See your medical practitioner.

Key words: Your health.

Polarity: Neutral.
Literal meaning: Never interpreted literally.

LEMON or **LIME:** Either of these fruits indicates that a grouchy, sour-dispositioned person will play a role in your life. This person will test your patience.

If this fruit is alone, you will be driven to the end of your patience and will soundly tell the person off in no uncertain terms.

If this fruit is coupled with any positive symbol, you will have sufficient patience to effectively overcome the person's negativism. If fact, your behavior will "sweeten" the person's disposition, and you both will emerge the better for having met.

If any negative symbol is coupled to this fruit, you need to be wary of this person because he or she is capable of harming you in some way. Your best bet is to avoid all contact with this person during the time period indicated.

Key words: Grouchy, sour-dispositioned person.
Polarity: Negative.
Literal meaning: Never interpreted literally.

LETTER, ALPHABETIC: Letters of the alphabet are always interpreted literally. Look to nearby symbols to get more complete information. For example, the letter "C" would be one initial of a friend's name if the "C" was coupled to a horse. If the "C" is in front or on top of the horse, it would be the friend's first name initial. If the "C" is behind or underneath the horse, it would be the last name initial.

The letter "P" coupled to an automobile could indicate the purchase of an automobile whose name begins with a "P" (Plymouth, Pontiac, Porsche, etc.).

Letters that are not related to any other symbols are always interpreted as the initials of some person's name. For example, the letter "J" standing all by itself near the cup rim about halfway around the cup would mean that someone with the initial "J" will play an important role in your life approximately six months from now.

Letters in a cup are always important. Minor events with people do not have the person's initials in the cup. Letters are always major.

Letters of the alphabet play another important role in the cup. Many symbols are to be interpreted literally if they are coupled with any letter of the alphabet. For example, a car symbolically means "domestic travel." However, if the car is coupled with any alphabetic letter, the car is to be interpreted literally as being a car and not as being domestic travel. The symbols that are affected in this manner are identified under their glossary definitions. Look up *Car* to get the idea.

Key words: Literal interpretation as the letter. Causes certain coupled symbols to be interpreted literally.

Polarity: Neutral.

Literal meaning: Alphabetic letters are always interpreted literally.

LETTER, MAIL: A postal letter (mail) means an important document. This could be a contract, a last will and testament, shares of stock or bonds, an important letter, or some other very important written document. This does not mean routine correspondence.

The letter indicates that you will be involved with an important document during the time period. Look to any coupled symbols for an indication of what it may be about, and whether you need to be extra cautious or not. For example, mail coupled with any negative symbol is a warning to be cautious. If coupled to a coiled snake, be wary of contracts that will likely cause you much trouble.

Coupled to any positive symbol, it is an indication that the document is beneficial.

If the letter (mail) is coupled with a dollar sign, money will be involved.

Key words: An important document.
Polarity: Neutral.
Literal meaning: A letter (mail) may or may not be interpreted literally. (Refer to explanation above.)

LIGHT BULB: A light bulb signifies energy. During the indicated time period, you will have an abundance of energy.

If the light bulb is coupled with another symbol, you will get a better idea of how you will expend your energy. For example, if coupled with a dollar sign, you will be engrossed in either spending or earning money or both.

If coupled with a positive symbol, you will achieve beneficial results with your energy. If coupled with a negative symbol, you will waste your energy.

If not coupled with any symbols, you will burn up your energy on a mixture of achievement and of waste.

Key words: An abundance of energy.

Polarity: Neutral.

Literal meaning: Never interpreted literally.

LIGHTNING BOLT: A lightning bolt indicates that you will be exceptionally alert and aware during the time period. You will learn quickly. You will understand clearly. You will be acutely aware of what others are doing and what they really mean when they say something. You will be aware when someone is trying to put something over on you. You will not be easily fooled by anyone or anything.

This would be an excellent time to take an adult education class or some other class because you will absorb everything quickly and completely.

Key words: Exceptionally alert and aware.

Polarity: Positive.

Literal meaning: If a lightning bolt is coupled with a numeral or an alphabetic letter, interpret the lightning bolt literally.

LION: A lion is a sign of fury. Either you will be furious with someone or someone will be furious with you. This is not just an emotional outburst of anger that will blow over. Fury implies deep hatred or resentment. Fury can trigger violence in some circumstances. Do not ignore this symbol because to do so could be tragic.

If the lion is not coupled with any other symbols, then you will be furious with someone. It will be up to you to curb the intensity of this fury because it could lead to violence.

If the lion is coupled with any positive symbol, someone will be furious with you, but it will not intensify to potential violence.

If the lion is coupled with a negative symbol, someone will be furious with you and it may escalate to the point of violence.

Since you know in advance that this is going to be a period of fury and potential violence, you have the responsibility to prevent it from happening or at least to keep it from becoming violent.

Key words: Fury and potential violence.
Polarity: Negative.
Literal meaning: Never interpreted literally.

LIPSTICK: Lipstick in a tea cup indicates vanity—yours. You are overly concerned about what people think of you and the superficial impression or appearance you make to others rather than on developing yourself into the kind of person that people will really like.

You put too much importance on superficial things like following a fad, going along with the gang because you want to be accepted, or being physically attractive. As a result, you are overlooking your inner development and are becoming a really shallow, uninteresting person.

If the lipstick is by itself in the cup, you will wake up in time to the fact that you really didn't fool anyone. You will be able to correct the situation if you really want to.

If the lipstick is coupled to a positive symbol, you will fool people for a long period of time before they get wise to your vanity and shallowness. When they do find out, most will desert you. However, at least one good friend will stick by you and help you reshape your life from the inside out (literally).

If the lipstick is coupled to a negative symbol, no one will be fooled by your superficiality except you. You will end up leading a lonely, shallow life unless you exert much determination to change. There won't be anyone to help you initially. You will be on your own. However, if you make a concerted effort to change, eventually someone will become your friend and help you.

Key words: Vanity. Superficiality. Shallowness.
Polarity: Negative.
Literal meaning: Never interpreted literally.

LIZARD: A lizard indicates a false fear. You'll find yourself fearing something during the time indicated, but it will be a fear that has no foundation in fact. The fear will be entirely in your mind.

For example, you fear you are going to lose your job because rumors say the company is on the verge of bankruptcy. The truth will be that it was just a rumor, not a fact, and your job will not be in jeopardy.

During this period, you will be well advised to curb your fears. If you find yourself worrying about something or fearing something, dismiss it without spending a great amount of time on it. Gear your thoughts to something constructive.

Key words: False fear.
Polarity: Negative.
Literal meaning: Never interpreted literally.

LOG: A log means a large gift. It can be either physically large, such as a refrigerator, or economically large, such as a thousand-dollar savings bond.

You will receive the gift if the log is coupled with any positive symbol, otherwise you will be the gift giver.

Key words: Large gift.
Polarity: Positive.
Literal meaning: Never interpreted literally.

LOLLIPOP: A lollipop indicates that a child, usually under the age of twelve, will play a significant role in your life during the time period. In any case, you will learn much from the encounter.

If the lollipop is by itself or is coupled with a positive symbol, it will be a beneficial experience. It will also be a pleasant experience if coupled with a positive symbol.

If coupled with a negative symbol, it will be an unpleasant experience.

Key words: A child under twelve years old.
Polarity: Neutral
Literal meaning: Never interpreted literally.

-*M*-

MAILBOX: This means that someone is expecting news from you. You will be aware that you need to give the news. Your delay in giving the news is causing the other person some anxiety.

If the mailbox is alone, the news you have to give won't be everything the other person needs to know, but you should not wait for more details. Tell what you know now because it will help the other person feel better.

If the mailbox is coupled with a positive symbol, it is good news that you have to give.

If the mailbox is coupled with a negative symbol, it is unpleasant news that you have to give. In any case, you should not delay in passing the news on.

Key words: Someone expects news from you.
Polarity: Neutral.
Literal meaning: Never interpreted literally.

MATCH: A match means that someone will impose on you—or at least attempt to impose on you.

If the match is coupled with a positive symbol, they will not be successful. You will firmly but politely turn the imposition attempt away and refuse to be "used" by the other person.

If the match is coupled with a negative symbol, the imposition will be successful because you didn't have the guts to assert your rights.

If the match is alone, you will allow the imposition this one time, but will let the other person know that this is not going to be a habit.

Key word: Imposition.
Polarity: Negative.
Literal meaning: Never interpreted literally.

MERMAID: You will be in a happy and playful mood during the time period indicated.

Other symbols, regardless of polarity, that are near the mermaid have no influence. You will be happy and playful even if your life's circumstances are difficult at the time. The mermaid helps you to cope by keeping you in a positive, joyful frame of mind for that time period.

Key words: Joyful and playful.
Polarity: Positive.
Literal meaning: Never interpreted literally.

MIRROR: A mirror indicates that now is an excellent time to take a good, honest look at yourself. Is your life going the way you want it? Are you satisfied? Do you like yourself? What do you want from life? What are your plans?

The mirror advises you to do a thorough self-examination over a several-week period during the time indicated in the cup. During this time you will be more inclined to be objective. As a result, you can make sound decisions and take actions to get every aspect of your life on the path you want.

Any symbols that may be coupled with the mirror will give you clues to things about yourself that need special consideration. For example, if a dog is coupled to the mirror you need to ask yourself questions such as "Do I have any real friends?" If not, "Why?" "What kind of friend am I?"

Key word: Self-examination.
Polarity: Positive.
Literal meaning: Never interpreted literally.

MONEY: Any symbols that look like coins or currency should be interpreted literally as money. If the money is not coupled to any other symbol, it means you will have sufficient means to live and pay your bills but not to save or to buy luxuries.

If the money is coupled to any positive symbol, you will have more than you need to live and can thus save some or afford some luxuries.

If the money is coupled to any negative symbol, you will need more money than you have.

Key word: Money.
Polarity: Neutral.
Literal meaning: Money is always interpreted literally.

MONKEY: A monkey indicates foolish behavior on your part. For instance, purchasing a luxury item that you can't afford, or marrying someone you don't love, etc.

If the monkey is coupled to any other symbol, you can get some clue as to what the foolish behavior might be concerned with. Otherwise, you only know that you will behave foolishly in some way—or perhaps in several ways—during the time period indicated.

Key words: Foolish behavior.

Polarity: Negative.
Literal meaning: Never interpreted literally.

MOON: The Moon is interpreted as "change." If the Moon is not coupled with other symbols, it simply indicates a period of important change in your life.

If the Moon is coupled with another symbol, you can tell more detail about the change. For example, if coupled with a desk or an anvil, it indicates a change in occupation or employment. In this example, it would mean you will become employed if you are currently unemployed, or if you are currently employed, you will either change jobs or become unemployed.

Key word: Change.
Polarity: Neutral.
Literal meaning: Never interpreted literally.

MOUNTAIN: A mountain represents a major challenge that you must deal with during the time indicated. It could be any sort of challenge: to master a new job; to overcome an illness or injury; or to win a competition.

If the mountain is coupled with another symbol, you will have more detail concerning the challenge.

Key words: A major challenge.
Polarity: Positive.
Literal meaning: If the mountain is coupled with a numeral or a letter of the alphabet, interpret the mountain literally.

MOUSE: A mouse is a nuisance that will pester you. It could be a person who is a nuisance. For example, an unwanted love interest who won't leave you alone.

It could be a situation that is a nuisance. For example, your car is being repaired and you have to take a bus to work which requires an extra two hours a day commuting time. In any event, it is a minor negative nuisance that will be short lived.

Be sure you interpret the symbol correctly as being a mouse. A rat and a mouse can look similar in a tea cup, but they have very different meanings (see *Rat*). The way to tell the difference is by the tail length. If it has no tail or a very short tail, it is a mouse. The rat will have a tail as long as, or longer than, its body.

Key words: A nuisance.

Polarity: Slightly negative.

Literal meaning: If the mouse is coupled with a numeral or an alphabetic letter, interpret the mouse literally.

MUSICAL INSTRUMENT: Any musical instrument denotes an innate musical ability in general, and a specific ability for the instrument shown. For example, a drum would indicate a special ability to play the drums. Certain instruments denote additional abilities as follows:

Piano: This indicates you have the ability to write songs and music.

Guitar: This indicates you have singing ability and could do well as a solo performer.

Wind instrument: A wind instrument signifies that you would perform best as a member of a group or band.

Violin: A violin indicates that you have extraordinary musical ability in general and have the potential of becoming a musical genius.

Key words for all: Musical ability.

Polarity for all: Positive.

Literal meaning for all: Never interpreted literally.

MUSICAL NOTE: One musical note signifies harmony in your life. Multiple notes signify internal harmony and strength bordering on sainthood.

If the multiple notes are coupled with any symbol that signifies another person, then you will be privileged to meet a highly developed, spiritual person who will have a profound effect on your life in some positive way.

Key word: Harmony.

Polarity: Positive.

Literal meaning: Never interpreted literally.

MUSTACHE: The interpretation of a mustache depends on whether it is in a man's tea cup or a woman's tea cup.

Man's cup: A mustache in a man's tea cup indicates good self-esteem, good personal hygiene, and self-respect.

More often than not, this also indicates the man is a loner—an independent thinker. He does not follow the crowd or conform to fads. He is confident, and does not turn to others for help or fulfillment. He feels complete within himself.

This symbol does not couple with any other symbol even if they are within a quarter-inch of each other. The mustache always stands alone in a man's cup.

Woman's cup: A mustache in a woman's tea cup indicates her desire to have a love affair with her ideal man. If the mustache is alone, she will have the desire, but it will not be fulfilled. If the mustache is coupled with any positive symbol, she will have the affair with enjoyable, beneficial results. If the mustache is coupled with any negative symbol, she will have the affair with disastrous results.

In any case, the affair is predicted in the tea cup. It may take place during that time, at some future time, or over a period of time. The actual affair is not limited to just the time period in the cup where the mustache appears.

Key words for all: Man's cup—good self-esteem, self-respect, hygiene, independent, loner, confident. Women's cup—desire for an affair.

Polarity for all: Man's cup—positive. Woman's cup—neutral.

Literal meaning for all: Never interpreted literally.

-N-

NAIL: A nail indicates a need for security. This pertains to security for your possessions, not for you personally; that is, security for your home, car, business (if you have one), and so forth.

The security implies adequate insurance, strong workable locks, fire and smoke alarms, burglar alarms, etc. If there is a nail in your tea cup, you should reassess your security situation and strengthen it if need be. If you take precautions, you can eliminate or lessen any potential problems.

Key words: Need for security.
Polarity: Negative.
Literal meaning: Never interpreted literally.

NECKTIE: A necktie indicates conformity in either a man or woman's
tea cup. It means you conform to
what others want even when you
would rather not. You are reluctant to

express your own thoughts and desires because you find
it less confronting to go along with the crowd.

If you want to feel better about yourself, you will
need to become more assertive in your feelings and
mannerisms. Start doing and saying what pleases you
rather than what pleases others. However, you have the
right to be whichever way you want. It is your choice.

Key word: Conformity.
Polarity: Slightly negative.
Literal meaning: Never interpreted literally.

NEEDLE: The interpretation of a needle depends on whether the needle has thread or not.

Without thread: A needle without thread indicates that you will have to make a major decision during the time period indicated. If the needle is coupled to other symbols, you can get a clue as to what the decision involves.

With thread: A needle and thread signifies that you will have a wish fulfilled during the time period indicated. This does not mean you should start making wild, irrational wishes on the premise that they will be filled for you. Rather, this symbol implies that some realistic, sincere wish will be granted.

Key words for all: Without thread—a major decision. With thread—a wish fulfilled.
Polarity for all: Positive.
Literal meaning for all: Never interpreted literally.

NEST: A bird's nest indicates your need for emotional security. You need love, warmth, friendship, a comforting home base. You need to be wanted and appreciated. These are things that are occupying much of your thoughts and concerns. You currently are not happy with the status of your emotional life.

If the nest is alone, you will find your emotional security, but not for a while yet, probably not for another year or more, but you will find it.

If the nest is coupled with any positive symbol, you will find your emotional security soon—within a year at the most, probably within a few months.

If the nest is coupled with any negative symbol, you are not likely to find your emotional security at all. In fact, if coupled with some of the more treacherous negative symbols such as a bat, rat, or coiled snake, you could be deluded into thinking you have found your emotional security only to have it turn to bitter hurt and disappointment.

Key words: Need for emotional security.
Polarity: Neutral.
Literal meaning: Never interpreted literally as a nest.

NOOSE: A noose in a cup indicates that the person is in danger of taking some action that they will ultimately regret. During the period indicated in the cup, the person should take great care in making all decisions so as to avoid problems. The adage "act in haste, repent at leisure" is in effect here. Caution is the order of the day.

If the noose is coupled with any negative symbol, the outcome of a bad decision could be quite disastrous to the person, even life threatening if coupled with an extremely negative symbol such as three sixes (6 6 6) or a bat (the animal, not the baseball bat).

If the noose is coupled with a positive symbol, the outcome of a bad decision will be less serious, perhaps causing a modest loss of money, loss of a friendship, loss of a job, etc.

Key words: Danger of making bad decisions.
Polarity: Negative.
Literal meaning: Never interpreted literally.

NUMERAL: All numerals (numbers) are always interpreted literally; that is, seeing a 3 means the number three; a 7, the number seven, etc.

Look for other symbols near the numeral in order to determine what the numeral applies to. For example, a 3 next to a clover could mean that the number three would be your lucky number during the indicated time period. That might be a good time to purchase three lottery tickets.

Numerals always pertain to some important or major event, and they play another important role in the tea cup. Many symbols are to be interpreted literally if they are coupled with any numeral. For example, a horse symbolically means "a friend." However, if the horse is coupled with any numeral, the horse is to be interpreted literally as a horse and not as a friend. (The symbols that are affected in this manner are identified under their glossary definitions. Look up *Horse* to get the idea.)

Key words: Literal interpretation as a numeral. Causes certain coupled symbols to be interpreted literally.

Polarity: Neutral.
Literal meaning: Numerals are always interpreted literally.

NURSING BOTTLE: A nursing bottle indicates a spoiled person. This person is you unless the bottle is coupled to some symbol indicating another person such as a figure of a person, a dog, horse, etc.

During the time period indicated, you will be in a situation in which your being spoiled is challenged by someone else. You will have the opportunity to face the fact that you are spoiled and to take mature action to grow up emotionally, or you can act like a spoiled brat and remain emotionally immature. The choice is yours.

Key words: Spoiled brat. Emotionally immature.
Polarity: Negative.
Literal meaning: Never interpreted literally.

-O-

OARS: Oars signify that you are progressing toward your goals and new experiences. One oar means you are making headway, slowly but surely. Two oars mean that you are making headway smoothly, steadily, and reasonably quickly.

If the oar (or oars) is coupled with any positive symbol, your success will come with minimal delay or problems.

If coupled with any negative symbol, your path to success will be delayed and driven off course before you finally reach your goal.

In any case, you will encounter new experiences from which you can learn, enjoy, and mature in wisdom.

Key words: Progressing toward your goals and new experiences.

Polarity: Positive.

Literal meaning: Never interpreted literally.

ORANGE (FRUIT): An orange is seen in the tea cup as an orange slice, not as a whole orange. This is because it is not possible to distinguish between a whole orange and a ball, which has an entirely different interpretation. Orange slices are not often seen in tea cups.

The meaning of an orange slice is "cheerfulness." In the time period indicated, you will be exceptionally cheerful just about all the time. You will see humor in situations that would normally cause you to complain or get angry. This will be a happy period for you for no particular reason except that you feel happy.

The polarity of nearby symbols have no effect one way or the other on the meaning of the orange slice.

Key word: Cheerfulness.

Polarity: Positive.

Literal meaning: Never interpreted literally.

-*P*-

PADLOCK: A padlock indicates that the trouble or problems which you have been experiencing will suddenly subside and go away. When you enter the time period indicated in the cup, you will experience a very quick change from problems to a quiet, problem-free life.

If the padlock is coupled with any positive symbol, the freedom from those particular problems will be permanent. Of course, you may eventually encounter other problems or trouble in your life, but not in this time period and not from the same problems.

If the padlock is coupled with any negative symbol, your freedom from those particular problems will last only for a couple weeks, and then they will return.

Key words: Trouble subsiding.
Polarity: Positive.
Literal meaning: Never interpreted literally.

PAIL: A pail indicates that you should "bail out" of some personal situation as quickly as you possibly can. For example, you are involved in a no-win relationship and you should get out now before you end up getting seriously hurt emotionally, financially, or physically. Perhaps you are involved in some financial venture that will collapse around you if you don't get out now.

If the pail is coupled with any positive symbol, you will have the foresight and the guts to bail out. You will get out in time before disaster falls.

If the pail is coupled with any negative symbol, you will get seriously hurt if you fail to heed the warning within the time period indicated. Usually this means within a two-week period of the time the pail appears in the cup.

If it is a large pail that covers several weeks by itself, you have a couple additional weeks to take your "bail out" action. If it is a small pail, you have less time, perhaps only a few days to a week.

Key words: Time to bail out of a situation.

Polarity: Negative.

Literal meaning: Never interpreted literally.

PAN: A pan indicates that you will be dealing with hunger during the time period indicated in the tea cup.

If the pan is by itself or coupled with any positive symbol, you will be helping someone who is hungry. Perhaps you will be involved in a food drive to help poor or elderly people. Perhaps you will buy a meal for someone who is down and out. Perhaps you will donate money to buy food for some charitable organization or you will do volunteer work such as for a "meals on wheels" program.

If the pan is coupled with any negative symbol, you are the one who will be hungry and in need of help.

This symbol does not indicate how long the hunger will last, only that you will be involved with it during, or at the start of, the indicated time period.

Key word: Hunger.
Polarity: Negative.
Literal meaning: Never interpreted literally.

PAPER: Paper is difficult to discern in a tea cup. It may appear to be a newspaper, a roll of some sort of paper, or a sheet of paper. You have to rely heavily on your intuition when you declare that a symbol is paper because it can appear to be something else. For instance, a roll of paper can look very much like a log, which has a very different meaning. This is another reason it would be wise for you to keep notes about your tea leaf predictions; it helps you to learn.

Paper indicates that some written document will play an important role in your life during the time period indicated. It does not indicate what kind of document. Look to any symbols that may be coupled with the paper in order to obtain a more complete picture.

If the paper is coupled with any negative symbol, do not sign any contract, purchase agreement, or other legal papers during the time period because it will end disastrously for you. Postpone signing legal documents until several weeks after the time period.

Key words: Important documents.
Polarity: Neutral.
Literal meaning: Never interpreted literally.

PEN: A pen signifies any occupation that primarily deals with written communication such as writing (author), secretarial, editing, clerical, court reporting, copywriting, etc.

If the pen is by itself or coupled with any positive symbol, such an occupation would be good for you. You should consider changing your occupation to such a field if you are not already so employed.

If you are already in such an occupation, it indicates that it is a good choice and you should stay in it rather than switch to an entirely different line of work.

If the pen is coupled with any negative symbol, it indicates that such an occupation would not be in your best interest. You would be wise to change if you are already in such an job. Do not seek work in such an occupation.

Key words: Occupation in written communications.
Polarity: Neutral.
Literal meaning: Never interpreted literally.

PENIS: The interpretation of a penis depends on whether the symbol is in a woman's tea cup or a man's tea cup.

In a man's cup: A penis by itself signifies that the man is egotistical, chauvinistic, self-centered, obsessed with sexual matters, and has a shallow character.

If the penis is coupled with any positive symbol, the meaning is the same as when the penis is alone with the following additional meaning: the man is personable and is able to cover up his true nature to a large degree. As a result, most people perceive him as being a nice guy.

If the penis is coupled with any negative symbol, the meaning is the same as when the penis is alone with the following additional meaning: the man's sexual obsession is perverted, and his personality is such that people don't like being around him. He is perceived by others as being a creep. Since this man signifies you, you need to seriously re-evaluate yourself and take decisive steps to bring yourself into balance if you want to have a happy, fulfilling life.

In extreme cases, such as when the penis is coupled with a highly negative symbol like a coiled snake or a rat, you need to seek professional help.

In a woman's cup: A penis by itself signifies that the woman is confident, independent, self-disciplined, in control, and does not allow herself to be intimidated or misused by men.

If the penis is coupled with any positive symbol, the meaning is the same as when the penis is alone with the following additional meaning: the woman is personable and is perceived by others as being warm, sincere, and a person others like to be around.

If the penis is coupled with any negative symbol, the meaning is the same as when the penis is alone with the following additional meaning: the woman is perceived by others as being cold, hard, and heartless. People feel uncomfortable around her.

Key words for all: Man's cup—egotistical, obsessed with sex. Woman's cup—confident, independent, disciplined.

Polarity for all: Man's cup—highly negative. Woman's cup—highly positive.

Literal meaning for all: Never interpreted literally.

PERSON: Any figure of a person in your tea cup represents someone other than yourself. It may be someone you already know or it may be someone you don't know yet. Sometimes you can tell whether the figure is male or female; interpret these literally.

Any symbols that are coupled with the person are to be interpreted as applying to that person, not to yourself.

Key words: Some person other than yourself.

Polarity: Neutral.

Literal meaning: A figure of a person is always interpreted literally as being a person other than yourself. The gender is also interpreted literally.

PIG: A pig means "greed." If the pig is alone (that is, not coupled with any other symbol) it indicates that you have a singular greed that is almost an obsession with you.
For example: greedy for money, greedy for food, etc.

If the pig is coupled with any positive symbol, you rationalize your greed by telling yourself that you need it, or you are trying to get ahead, or you are just trying to take care of your family. You will come up with some seemingly logical excuse for your greed rather than recognize it for what it is.

If the pig is coupled with any negative symbol, you are greedy for many things just for the sake of getting more than what the other person has. You are obsessed with getting everything you can however you can, just because you want it.

This is one of the most detrimental symbols to have in a tea cup because a greedy person rarely changes to any significant degree.

If the pig is coupled with one of the more powerful positive symbols such as a cross or a church steeple, there is reasonable hope that you will overcome your greed and find more balance in your life.

Key word: Greed.

Polarity: Highly negative.

Literal meaning: Never interpreted literally.

PIN: A pin indicates that you will be getting a new job very soon, usually within two weeks to two months. This could be a new job at your current place of employment, or it could be a job with a new employer.

If the pin is by itself, the new job is most likely to be with a new employer.

If coupled with a positive symbol, the new job is most likely to be a promotion with your current employer.

If coupled with a negative symbol, the new job will most likely be lower paying or a lower level job than the one you currently have. It could be either at your current place of employment or at a new place.

Key words: New job.
Polarity: Neutral.
Literal meaning: Never interpreted literally.

PIPE (FOR SMOKING): A pipe (for smoking) indicates a reconciliation. This usually means that you will make peace with someone with whom you had a falling out. The reconciliation will either take place during the time period indicated or within a month after that.

If the pipe is by itself, you will accept the reconciliation reluctantly and with reservation. Things will not return to the way they were before, but you will maintain a semblance of friendship.

If the pipe is coupled to any positive symbol, you welcome the reconciliation joyfully, and it will be successful. Things will rapidly go back to the way they were before.

If coupled with any negative symbol, the reconciliation will be superficial only and will not last long.

Key word: Reconciliation.
Polarity: Positive.
Literal meaning: Never interpreted literally.

PIPE (WATER): Someone will be bringing the person information that will be vitally important and beneficial to the person and his or her life.

This symbol is not affected by other symbols except numerals and alphabetic characters. Interpret a water pipe literally as being a water pipe if it is coupled with a numeral or alphabetic character. If interpreted literally as being a water pipe, it usually is forecasting water problems in the home or car.

Key words: Vital, beneficial information. Water problems if interpreted literally.

Polarity: Positive.

Literal meaning: Interpreted literally as being a water pipe if it is coupled with a numeral or a letter.

PLOW: A plow in your tea cup indicates that you are in for a struggle during the time period indicated.

If the plow is by itself, your struggle will most likely be with yourself, fighting your own negativism, or struggling to keep a positive attitude about your job, your life situation, your abilities to cope, and to succeed. It will be a period of inner conflict, marked with moments of self-doubt and disillusionment.

If the plow is coupled with any positive symbol, your struggle will most likely be in the workplace where you are struggling competitively to get promoted, to get a salary increase, to get more sales, and so forth.

If the plow is coupled with any negative symbol, your struggle is most likely to be a physical one. For example, battling against an illness; struggling against some physical endurance such as a competitive sporting encounter; struggling for survival, such as in a blizzard, a flood, etc. In some extreme cases, you could be struggling against another person for your survival.

Key word: Struggle.
Polarity: Negative.
Literal meaning: Never interpreted literally.

POWER LINES: This symbol is
not often seen in a tea cup. It is a
powerful symbol that indicates
you will have enormous resources
at your disposal for whatever pur-
pose you desire. These resources are both personal as
well as external. If it is personal, you will have physical
stamina, mental sharpness, keen intuition, etc. If it is
external, you will have material resources like money,
property, political or social influence, etc.

Other symbols have no influence on the power lines.

Key words: Enormous resources.
Polarity: Highly positive.
Literal meaning: Never interpreted literally.

PRETZEL: A pretzel signifies complexities in your life
that will confuse, perplex, and frustrate you. Nothing will
be simple. Ordinary tasks will somehow become difficult
or exceptionally time consuming. Communications will
get fouled up. For example, you make a date for Friday,
and the other person thought you said Saturday. If you
are taking a motor trip, you will get lost, or have to take a
lengthy detour, etc.

This will be a trying period for you. Fortunately, the
pretzel never indicates anything serious, just frustrating.

If the pretzel is by itself, this frustrating period will last about one to two weeks.

If the pretzel is coupled with any positive symbol, the period will last less than a week.

If the pretzel is coupled with any negative symbol, the period could last up to a month.

In any case, there will be no serious harm done except possibly to your patience and nervous system.

Key words: Period of frustrations and complexities.

Polarity: Negative.

Literal meaning: Never interpreted literally.

PUMP: A pump indicates that you will encounter a person who will ask you many questions.

If the pump is by itself, the person will be just plain nosy. The person will try to pry into your personal business with the intent to gather something to gossip about. How successful this person will be in "pumping" you depends on whether you allow it or not.

If the pump is coupled to any positive symbol, the person will be "pumping" you for information in a sincere effort to learn. You will be in a teaching role, and the person will be in a student role. For example, you are assigned to "break in" a new hire.

If the pump is coupled to any negative symbol, you will be "pumped" for information in the investigative sense. For example, you are in the witness chair in a trial and are being questioned by an attorney, or perhaps the police are questioning you regarding some situation.

Key words: You are being questioned.

Polarity: Neutral.
Literal meaning: Never interpreted literally.

PURSE: A purse refers to your financial situation. If the purse is by itself, it means that your financial situation is stable and adequate to meet your obligations.

If the purse is coupled with a positive symbol, your financial situation is quite good. You are financially sound, and have enough to afford just about anything you want.

If the purse is coupled with any negative symbol, your financial situation is tight. You will need to trim your spending to the barest survival level. In extreme cases, such as being coupled with a coiled snake or a rat, you could become destitute.

Key words: Pertains to your financial situation.
Polarity: Neutral.
Literal meaning: Never interpreted literally.

-*Q*-

QUILL: A quill signifies that you need to get back to the basics. You have allowed your lifestyle to become so opulent that you have lost sight of the real value and joy in living. You have become too concerned about status, and have forgotten your humble roots.

This is a period in which you need to strive to put yourself and your lifestyle back into balance. You need to get back in touch with those things and those people that were once so important to you. Eliminate the superficial icons you have allowed to possess you, and replace them with truth, integrity, honesty, and genuineness.

The polarity of other nearby symbols does not have any influence on the quill.

Key words: Need to get back to the basics.
Polarity: Negative.
Literal meaning: Never interpreted literally.

-*R*-

RABBIT: A rabbit in a tea cup indicates a carefree person. A carefree person is one who does not take life or oneself too seriously.

If the rabbit is not coupled to any other symbol indicating another person, then the carefree person is you. The rabbit by itself indicates that you are a carefree person with balance. This is a good sign because you will know how to enjoy life while still facing up to your responsibilities.

If the rabbit is coupled to any positive symbol, it indicates that you need to become a more carefree person. You take things much too seriously, and you need to loosen up a little and learn how to enjoy life more.

If the rabbit is coupled to any negative symbol, it indicates that you are too much in the carefree direction.

You neglect or ignore responsibilities in favor of play and self-indulgence. You need to develop a stronger sense of responsibility.

Key words: Carefree person.
Polarity: Mildly positive.
Literal meaning: Never interpreted literally.

RADIO: If you see a radio in your tea leaves, it means you will hear some news or information that will have a profound effect on you. The information can be via a telephone, a face-to-face conversation or an overheard one, a recording, or a radio. For example, you might listen to a self-help audio cassette tape that helps you alter your life in a way you consider better.

If the radio is coupled with any negative symbol, the news or information will not be pleasant or joyful.

If coupled with any positive symbol, the news or information will be pleasant or joyful.

If the radio is by itself, the news or information is most likely to be of an unemotional nature which you merely assimilate and use.

Key words: Hear information that will have a profound effect on you.
Polarity: Positive.
Literal meaning: Never interpreted literally.

RAINBOW: You are not able to see colors in a cup of tea leaves so you don't literally see a rainbow of seven colors. The rainbow is shown in tea leaves as being a high arc in the shape of a rainbow. A rainbow means that the most difficult part of your life is over now, and the future will be much more pleasant and beautiful.

If there is any symbol indicating money near either end of the rainbow, your future will be exceptionally prosperous.

The polarity of nearby symbols has no effect one way or the other on the rainbow.

Key words: The most difficult part of your life is over.

Polarity: Highly positive.

Literal meaning: Never interpreted literally.

RAKE: The rake signifies that during the time period indicated, you will be involved in some very serious searching. It could be searching for a missing person, it might be serious soul searching for a major decision that will significantly affect the rest of your life, or some other serious searching. In any case, it will not be superficial such as searching for a parking place at the supermarket.

If the rake is by itself, the searching will be successful but not easy. If the rake is coupled with any positive symbol, the searching will be relatively easy and of short duration, and will be successful.

If the rake is coupled with any negative symbol, the searching will be exceptionally difficult and may be unsuccessful. If coupled with a negative symbol that is not very powerfully negative such as a bee, a pretzel, or a lizard, the searching could be successful but difficult.

Key words: Serious searching.
Polarity: Neutral.
Literal meaning: Never interpreted literally.

RAT: A rat indicates a treacherous, dishonest, evil person who will enter your life during the time period indicated. For example, someone steals your car or burglarizes your house, or someone tries to cheat you in a business deal, or someone deliberately deceives you in some way, etc. This is not a symbol to be taken lightly.

Be sure you interpret the symbol correctly as being a rat. A mouse and a rat can look similar in a tea cup, but they have very different meanings (see *Mouse*). The way to tell the difference is by the tail length. If it has no tail or a very short tail, it is a mouse. The rat will have a tail as long as, or longer than, its body.

If the rat is coupled with any positive symbol, you will not be physically harmed by the treacherous person.

If the rat is coupled with any negative symbol, you are in danger of being physically harmed by this person.

In all cases, you need to beware of this person because you will suffer in some way because of him or her—financially, emotionally, etc.

Key words: Treacherous, dishonest person.

Polarity: Highly negative.

Literal meaning: If the rat is coupled with a numeral or an alphabetic letter, interpret the rat literally.

RING: A ring is the symbol of marriage. If the ring is not broken, it indicates that a marriage will take place.

If the ring has a fairly large, clean break in it, it indicates a breakup of a marriage either by divorce or death. If it is a thin break like a hairline crack, it means only a separation. Many thin breaks mean many separations. Many large breaks, many marriages ending in divorce or death. The number of breaks indicates the number of breakups or separations.

Look for other symbols close to the ring in order to get a more complete picture. For example, the numeral "2" appearing close to a solid ring would mean two marriages. A dollar sign next to a broken ring would likely mean a costly divorce.

If any positive symbol is coupled to a solid ring, it indicates a good marriage. If coupled to a ring that has thin breaks in it, the separations will be due to external factors such as the husband being drafted into the army and not because of any marital problems. If coupled to a broken ring, the breakup will be most likely due to a friendly divorce or perhaps to death. In the case of death, it would have been a good marriage.

If any negative symbol is coupled to a solid ring, it indicates a stormy, troubled, possibly violent marriage. If coupled to a ring with thin breaks, the separations will be due to the violent nature of the marriage. If coupled to a ring with a large break, a messy divorce or a death.

Key word: Marriage.
Polarity: Positive.
Literal meaning: Never interpreted literally.

ROCKING CHAIR: This is a symbol that most people would probably like to see in their tea cup because it indicates a long life. If the rocking chair is by itself, you  can expect a long life (seventy years or more) and reasonably good health most of the time.

If coupled with a positive symbol, you can expect better health, resources, and enjoyment than most.

If coupled with a negative symbol, you can expect the reverse: poorer health, fewer resources, and less enjoyment than most.

Key words: Long life.
Polarity: Positive.
Literal meaning: Never interpreted literally.

ROOF: A roof implies protection to you, your family, and your possessions. There is no negative action, situation, or development that can harm you in any way during the time period that a roof appears. The roof is not affected by the polarity of nearby symbols.

If the roof is so large that it spans into several time zones of the cup, then it indicates protection for you, your family, and your possessions for your entire life.

Key words: Protection for you, your family, and your possessions.

Polarity: Highly positive.

Literal meaning: Never interpreted literally.

ROPE: The interpretation of a rope is "capture." To determine just what capture means, you are required to analyze the entire cup to some degree. For example, suppose the cup in general indicated a person who was striving to get ahead by hard work and study. Then capture would probably mean that the person would capture success, especially if the rope is not coupled with a negative symbol.

If the cup indicated a person who was dishonest, lazy, etc., then capture might well mean that this person will be arrested at some point for breaking the law.

Look closely at all nearby symbols, their meanings and their polarity in order to see just how "capture" fits in.

A rope, in my opinion, is the most difficult of all symbols to interpret. It helps to have a lot of intuition (or a quartz crystal—see the Appendix).

Key word: Capture.
Polarity: Neutral.
Literal meaning: Never interpreted literally.

RULER: This measuring instrument indicates that during the time period indicated in the tea cup, you will be exceptionally conscious of time.

If the ruler is by itself, you will be either planning or doing something in which time is a key element. For example, you are scheduling a series of public appearances for a politician to coincide with state caucuses.

If the ruler is coupled with any positive symbol, then during the time period indicated, time will seem to fly by so fast that you won't get all the things done that you want to get done.

If coupled with any negative symbol, time will seem to drag for you. Each day will seem to be an eternity.

Key words: Conscious of time.
Polarity: Neutral.
Literal meaning: Never interpreted literally.

-S-

SADDLE: A saddle indicates that you will be protected from your own poor judgment. For example, suppose you invested in a get-rich-quick scheme that went sour. Originally you would lose all your money. However, if there is a saddle in your cup, some circumstance or situation will arise that will keep you from losing all your money even though others do lose theirs.

Usually you always have to "pay the piper" when you act with poor judgment. In other words, you generate a certain negative energy that must be offset—karma.

The saddle in your tea cup indicates that you will not have to experience that karma.

Understand this: the saddle does not offset all your karma. It only offsets the karma you generate from one act of poor judgment during the time period indicated in the tea cup. For example, if the saddle appeared anywhere in the third month section of the tea cup, the saddle would protect you from the negative karma you generate from one act of poor judgment committed during the third month. If the saddle appeared in a portion of the sixth and seventh month area of the cup, you would be protected from the negative karma you generate from one act of poor judgment committed during the sixth and seventh month, and so on. The protection from that karma is effective for the rest of your life.

The saddle implies that you will indeed perform some act of poor judgment during that time period. That is why the saddle appears. Nothing ever appears in the tea cup without good reason.

If you are forewarned by the saddle, you may well prevent the karma because you will know that you will likely act with poor judgment. Therefore, all you need to do is to think clearly before you act during the time period. Don't act in haste in any matter during the time period. Be cautious. This is good advice anytime, but especially so when a saddle appears.

Key words: Protection from your own poor judgment.
Polarity: Highly positive.
Literal meaning: Never interpreted literally.

SAFE: If you have a safe in your tea cup, you are guaranteed sufficient financial and personal security for the rest of your life.

If the safe is by itself, your security will be comfortably sufficient. If the safe is coupled with any positive symbol, your security will be much more than you will ever need.

If coupled with any negative symbol, your security will be just barely sufficient—enough for paying your bills, tending to your health, and feeding and clothing you, but little or nothing left over for frills or luxuries.

In any case, not to worry—you will be independently secure. You won't have to rely on charity, relatives, social programs, etc.

Key words: Independently secure for life.
Polarity: Highly positive.
Literal meaning: Never interpreted literally.

SCALES: These scales are the kind that portray a bar with a balance plate on each end of the bar. When both plates are the same height, the scales are balanced. If one plate is lower than the other, the scales are out of balance. The interpretation of scales is dependent on whether the scales you see in the tea cup are balanced or unbalanced.

In balance: Balanced scales indicate that you are reasonably in balance mentally, physically, spiritually, and in all aspects of your life. This puts you in perfect condition to forge ahead toward whatever goals you have because you will certainly succeed.

Unbalanced: Unbalanced scales indicate that some aspect of you or your life is sufficiently out of balance and you need to make yourself aware of it and work to correct it. It would be unwise to forge ahead toward your goals until you first get yourself into balance because you will likely fail if you are out of balance.

If there are any symbols coupled with the unbalanced scales, you may be able to determine just which aspect of you or your life needs to be corrected.

For example, unbalanced scales that are coupled with a dollar sign indicate that your financial situation is not in the proper condition for you to forge ahead toward your goals. Unbalanced scales coupled with a fly indicate that your health needs to be tended to now.

Key words for all: Balanced scales—you and your life are in balance. Unbalanced scales—some aspect of you or your life is out of balance and needs to be corrected now.

Polarity for all: Positive.

Literal meaning for all: Never interpreted literally.

SCISSORS: Scissors indicate that you are going to experience a major disappointment during the time period indicated.

If any symbols are coupled with the scissors, you can get some idea what the disappointment is concerned with. For example, scissors coupled with a heart shape indicates that you will be disappointed in love.

Key word: Disappointment.

Polarity: Negative.

Literal meaning: Never interpreted literally.

SCOOTER: The scooter signifies that you will make progress in your work or other activities by your own efforts, and you will have a good time doing it. You won't get much, if any, help from anyone, but you won't care. You know you can do it yourself, and you are having fun as a bonus. You will be enjoying the best of two worlds—play and work.

The polarity of nearby symbols has no effect on the scooter. Of course, the meaning of nearby symbols does have an effect on the scooter. For example, a bee coupled to the scooter would mean that people at work will gossip about you; however, it won't have any detrimental effect at all. The gossip is there, but you just keep on progressing without problems. The gossip won't even dampen your fun.

Key words: Progress by your own efforts and having a
   good time doing it.
Polarity: Positive.
Literal meaning: Never interpreted literally.

SEA HORSE: The sea horse pertains to family strength and unity. If the sea horse is by itself, you will have to exert personal influence and guidance to have a strong, united family. You will be the focal point of the family. How you accept your role and responsibilities will determine whether the family is united or fragmented.

If coupled with any positive symbol, your family will be naturally strong and united with all members contributing to the well-being of the family unit.

If the sea horse is coupled with any negative symbol, there will be at least one divisive person (perhaps you) in the family who causes problems, disruption, and fragmentation. As long as this person (or persons) is included in family affairs, there will never be harmony.

Key words: Pertains to the family.
Polarity: Mildly positive.
Literal meaning: Never interpreted literally.

SHEEP: The sheep symbolizes passiveness, non-aggressiveness, calmness, gentleness.

In the tea cup, this means you will be faced with a difficult situation in which you must act and react as a sheep if you want to triumph; that is, you must maintain a low profile, be gentle, and non-aggressive. You must not fight back. You must remain passive. If you do not act as a sheep in this situation, you will not win.

The opposite of sheep is goat (see *Goat*). In difficult situations there are times when it's best to act as a sheep. Other times it is best to act as a goat. Let the tea cup be your guide.

Be sure you interpret the symbol correctly as being a sheep. A lamb can look very similar to a sheep, but the lamb has a slightly different meaning. (See *Lamb.*) If the symbol is small and lean with no tail (usually), it is a lamb. If it is a little fat, mature looking, and has a tail (usually), it is a sheep.

Key words: Passive. Non-aggressive. Calm. Low profile.
Polarity: Positive.
Literal meaning: Never interpreted literally.

SHEPHERD'S STAFF: This symbol means that no matter what sort of difficulty you get into, you will be taken care of by some benefactor.

For example, if someone were robbing you, a policeman would show up to protect you and apprehend the robber. If you were injured in a car accident by yourself in the middle of the night on a deserted road, the next car to come along would contain a physician who would help you, and so forth.

The polarity of nearby symbols has no effect on the shepherd's staff. The protection offered by the shepherd's staff is for your lifetime.

Key words: You'll be taken care of in difficult times.
Polarity: Highly positive.
Literal meaning: Never interpreted literally.

SHIELD: A warrior's shield indicates that you will encounter a situation during the indicated time period in which you will have to defend yourself. This could mean defending yourself in a court of law. It could mean defending your ideas. It could mean physically defending yourself from potential harm or in some sort of contest.

If any symbols are coupled with the shield, you may get some idea of what the defense will be about.

If the shield is coupled with any positive symbol, you will have a clear-cut win.

If the symbol is coupled with any negative symbol, you will experience a clear-cut loss.

If the shield is by itself, you will win a partial victory.

Key words: Need to defend yourself.
Polarity: Slightly negative.
Literal meaning: Never interpreted literally.

SHOE: A shoe means that you are going to have to increase your effort if you want to achieve your goals. The implication is that you have been doing things halfheartedly and even slacking off at times.

There are no free rides, but you have been acting as if you thought there were. Start buckling down and exercising self-discipline and plain old hard work. Otherwise, you will just be an "also ran" rather than a "winner."

Key words: Increase your effort.
Polarity: Slightly positive.
Literal meaning: Never interpreted literally.

SHOVEL: A shovel pertains to any occupation that relies primarily on physical effort rather than on mental effort.

A shovel that is coupled with any positive symbol indicates that you will do best in an occupation that involves a balance of physical effort and mental effort. For example, occupations like police officer, plumber, construction, most sports, etc.

A shovel that is alone in the tea cup indicates you would do best in any occupation that involves mostly physical effort with minimal mental effort. For example, occupations like a professional mover, longshoreman, housekeeper, postal carrier, professional model, etc.

A shovel that is coupled with any negative symbol indicates that you would do best in an occupation that involves minimal physical effort and maximum mental effort. For example, occupations like a lawyer, writer, accountant, teacher, etc.

Key words: Pertains to occupations involving physical effort.

Polarity: Positive.

Literal meaning: Never interpreted literally.

SICKLE: A sickle indicates illness. Unless the sickle is coupled with some symbol that indicates another person, you are the person who will be ill during the indicated time.

If the sickle is by itself, you will be ill enough to stay in bed a day or two but not be hospitalized.

If the sickle is coupled with any positive symbol, you will probably be able to continue working and to carry out your daily responsibilities. You will just feel poorly for a few days or a week.

If the sickle is coupled with any negative symbol, you will be quite ill and may even have to be hospitalized. You will not be able to function normally every day until the illness is overcome.

Key word: Illness.

Polarity: Negative.

Literal meaning: Never interpreted literally.

SKATEBOARD: A skateboard means that you are entirely on your own. You will succeed or fail depending on your own skill, power, and effort. There will be no help or support from anyone.

If the skateboard is coupled with any negative symbol, there will be forces that will actively try to cause you to fail. However, the negative forces will not be the cause of your failure if you do fail. You alone are responsible for your success or failure in the situation you will be dealing with during the time period in which the skateboard appears.

Key words: Entirely on your own.
Polarity: Positive.
Literal meaning: Never interpreted literally.

SKATES: This symbol is nearly identical to skateboard. (See *Skateboard.*) The difference in the two is that skates indicate you have a slightly better chance of succeeding because you will have more self-confidence than you will have if a skateboard symbol appears. Otherwise, the two symbols are identical in meaning.

Key words: Entirely on your own.
Polarity: Positive.
Literal meaning: Never interpreted literally.

SKELETON: A skeleton indicates that you have a secret that you do not want anyone to know about. It is something that you feel would, at least, greatly embarrass you and, at the most, devastate you if revealed.
This is a most important secret that you will go to great lengths to protect.

If the skeleton is alone in your tea cup, your secret will eventually be revealed, but it will not cause you the distress that you thought it would.

If the skeleton is coupled with any positive symbol, your secret is safe. It will never be uncovered.

If the skeleton is coupled with any negative symbol, your secret will be revealed, causing you great distress.

Key words: A great secret.
Polarity: Slightly negative.
Literal meaning: Never interpreted literally.

SKIS: Skis indicate that you are moving too fast in your life without paying close enough attention to details and responsibilities. These details and neglected responsibilities will soon catch up with you in an avalanche of trouble. By the time you reach the period indicated in the tea cup, the avalanche will already have been set into motion. You will not be able to escape it.

If the skis are alone, you will have to handle the trouble alone. Your friends will desert you.

If the skis are coupled with any positive symbol, your friends will stand by you as long as you make a sincere effort to conduct yourself with absolute integrity. If you don't, your friends will eventually give up on you.

If the skis are coupled with any negative symbol, your friends will turn on you when the trouble hits.

One example of what skis could indicate: you are so obsessed with getting ahead in your occupation that you play politics, make empty promises, use or misuse people, court favors from the "right" people, etc. As a result, you move up the ladder of promotion rapidly. You razzle-dazzle everyone—for a while. Then it all caves in on you because you built a career on nothing solid. Things rapidly go wrong. You get blamed for your poor judgment, for not taking care of details, for playing games instead of making solid contributions and accomplishments.

There are hundreds of other similar scenarios that skis could indicate.

Key words: Moving too fast without acting responsibly.
Polarity: Negative.
Literal meaning: Never interpreted literally.

SKULL: A skull signifies that you will be engaged in serious creative mental exercise during the time period indicated. This could be creative writing, creative art, brainstorming for the solution to a problem, devising some sort of complex plan, etc.

The polarity of nearby symbols does not have any effect one way or the other on a skull.

Key words: Serious creative mental exercise.
Polarity: Positive.
Literal meaning: Never interpreted literally.

SLED: A sled indicates a period of smooth sailing for you. Everything in your life will just smooth out. Everything will fall into place. No serious disruptions or problems.

This will be an excellent time for you to just rest up and enjoy doing very little. It will be a welcome change from the usual hubbub. Near the end of the period, you will actually start to become bored with the placidity.

The polarity of nearby symbols has no effect one way or the other on the meaning of the sled.

Key words: A period where there are no serious disruptions or problems.
Polarity: Positive.
Literal meaning: Never interpreted literally.

SNAKE: A snake in a tea cup can have two completely different meanings as follows:

Uncoiled: An uncoiled snake, one that is stretched out or appears to be crawling, is a sign of wisdom and strength. This is a good sign to have in your tea cup. For example, if you are ill and you have an uncoiled snake in your cup, you will have the strength to overcome the illness. If you are pondering a major decision (such as whether to get married, divorced, buy a car, etc.) you will have the wisdom to make the best decision.

Coiled: A coiled snake is always a sign of treachery. Almost always the treachery will come from someone you either don't know or wouldn't suspect, such as someone whom you think is your friend. When you have a coiled snake in your cup, you should always exercise extra vigilance and caution during the time period indicated.

For example, if the coiled snake is in the first quarter of the cup near the handle, be extra cautious for the next two weeks. If it is halfway around the cup and halfway down, be cautious during the sixth month from now, especially during the middle of the sixth month. Since your time estimates are going to be approximate, you would be wise to add a little extra time before and after the caution periods.

The coiled snake does not necessarily mean that treachery will absolutely happen. It is a warning that treacherous conditions are, or will be, present. If you exercise caution, you can often prevent the treachery from materializing into anything serious. For example, during the caution period, keep your house and car doors locked. Don't sleep with ground floor windows open. Don't flash money in public. Be wary of strangers and don't go on blind dates. Be careful with credit cards and be wary of salespeople and sales contracts. Be aware of everything that is happening around you. Even if you are just running into a convenience store for two minutes to get a newspaper, lock your car and take your keys.

Simply stated—exercise common sense and be on the defensive. Of course, all treachery is not always preventable. If a co-worker decides to lie to the boss about you, all you can do is deal with it when it happens. If your own conduct has been proper, someone's lying is not likely to cause permanent harm.

Key words for all: Coiled snake—treachery. Uncoiled snake—strength, wisdom.

Polarity for all: Coiled snake—highly negative. Uncoiled snake—highly positive.

Literal meaning for all: Never interpreted literally.

SPEAR: A spear means that you will experience heartache during the time period indicated. This could be any sort of heartache (the emotional kind, not physical) such as rejection by your lover, a death, loss of a pet, or loss of your money or other assets.

If the spear is alone, your heartache will be deep and last for a moderate period of time (a month to a year).

If other symbols are coupled with the spear, you can get an idea of what the heartache is about. For example, if the spear is coupled with a heart shape, you will suffer heartache over love.

If the spear is coupled with a positive symbol, your heartache will not be deep, and after a day or so it will quickly vanish.

If the spear is coupled with a negative symbol, your heartache will be severe and will last for years or even for your lifetime.

Key word: Heartache.

Polarity: Negative.

Literal meaning: Never interpreted literally.

SPIDER: A spider is a good luck symbol. The polarity of nearby symbols does not affect the spider in any way. No matter how dismal the rest of your tea cup may be, the spider offers a brief relief by bringing you a period of good luck. The period of good luck is usually about two weeks maximum around the time period in which the spider appears.

Usually the spider is not great good luck, but the good luck is sufficient that you will definitely notice it. For example, you get a better job or a salary increase. You may win something in the lottery, but it isn't likely to be over a hundred dollars or so.

Key words: Good luck.
Polarity: Positive.
Literal meaning: Never interpreted literally.

SPOOL: A spool means that you will have a secret revealed that you did not want anyone to know. No other symbol coupled with the spool has the power to overcome it—the secret will definitely be revealed no matter what. If the spool is alone, the revealed secret will cause some damage to you, but with time you will overcome it.

If any negative symbol is coupled with the spool, the revealed secret will be very damaging to you in some important way.

If any positive symbol is coupled with the spool, the revealed secret will be only slightly damaging to you, perhaps only embarrassing to you.

Key words: Secret revealed.
Polarity: Negative.
Literal meaning: Never interpreted literally.

SPOON: A spoon indicates training. If the spoon is by itself, you will give training of some kind to someone—you could be training just one person or a group. For example, you may be asked to train a new employee where you work or perhaps to teach a CPR class.

If the spoon is coupled with any positive symbol, you will receive some sort of training that you desire and that will help you.

If the spoon is coupled with any negative symbol, there will be training that you desire to give or to receive, but you will not be given the opportunity at this time.

Key word: Training.
Polarity: Positive.
Literal meaning: Never interpreted literally.

SPRINGS: A spring, which is a coil such as a bed spring, means "relaxation." During the time period indicated, you will have the opportunity for a great deal of relaxation; perhaps a vacation, or perhaps just a low-key period in which you have to do nothing urgent or pressing so you can relax.

Other nearby symbols have no effect on the spring. Interpret the spring as though it were by itself. No matter how much turmoil you may have in your life, when you hit the period where the spring appears, you will have relief and relaxation. The spring usually affects about a one to two week period.

Key word: Relaxation.
Polarity: Positive.
Literal meaning: Never interpreted literally.

SQUIRREL: A squirrel means "thrift" or "saving." The period of time in which the squirrel appears is an excellent time to open a savings account; or if you have a savings account, to increase the amount you deposit. This is an excellent time to plan a better budget and to curb unnecessary spending, to start saving for that "rainy day."

If the squirrel is by itself, it indicates that you are not irresponsible, but there is still room for enhancing your savings and trimming back frivolous spending.

If the squirrel is coupled with any positive symbol, it indicates that you do have a sound financial plan and a balanced approach to spending.

If the squirrel is coupled with any negative symbol, it indicates that your spending is out of control and your savings plan does not even exist. You need to develop discipline NOW or your future looks bleak indeed.

Key words: Saving. Thrift.
Polarity: Positive.
Literal meaning: Never interpreted literally.

STAIRS: Stairs indicate success. This is a powerful symbol that is not affected by the polarity of nearby symbols. If you have stairs in your tea cup, you are assured of success. Period! No ifs, ands or buts about it. You will succeed.

This is long-term lifetime success, not just a short-term one. There must be a minimum of two steps to be considered stairs. The number of steps indicates the relative degree of success. Two steps is moderate success;

three steps, above average success; four or more steps, great success.

Key word: Success.
Polarity: Highly positive.
Literal meaning: Never interpreted literally.

STAR: A star in your tea cup is a cardinal symbol of success. It always signifies personal recognition in some way. It is one of the most powerful of all positive symbols. It is even more powerful than "stairs" when it comes to guaranteeing success. (See *Stairs.*)

If the star is alone, it means you will achieve success in some manner that brings you into the public eye. This could be anything from being a national celebrity down to being elected to a local school board. The public will be aware of you in some measure, and whatever it is, you will be recognized and successful as an individual, not as a part of a group or organization.

If the star is coupled with another symbol, then your success will be in accordance with the blend of the meanings of the two symbols. For example, if the star is coupled with any wind instrument (musical), you will be a successful member of a musical group or band. If the star is coupled with a bat, you will successfully overcome treachery against you and will gain some sort of personal recognition in the process.

A star coupled with a desk indicates a successful career in which you are recognized and known—perhaps as a company manager.

When the star is coupled with symbols, you may not necessarily be in the public's eye, but you will be in the eye of those associated within your sphere of work or expertise.

However, a star alone guarantees public recognition.

The polarity of other symbols does not have any influence on the star.

Key words: Guaranteed success.

Polarity: Highly positive.

Literal meaning: If a star is coupled with a numeral or an alphabetic letter, interpret the star literally. Not the kind of star in the sky, but the kind of star that is a celebrity or famous person.

SUITCASE: A suitcase indicates that you will be moving your place of residence. The move will likely take place during the time period indicated or within two months maximum.

If the suitcase is by itself, the move will come on short notice and will be greeted with mixed blessings. For example, you are promoted at work and have to move to accept the new position.

If the suitcase is coupled with any positive symbol, it will be a move that you have planned and you look forward to. For example, a retirement village in Arizona.

If the suitcase is coupled with any negative symbol, it will be a move that you don't want to make and usually for unpleasant reasons. For example, you are unable to pay your rent and are evicted, or your marriage breaks up, and you must get out.

Key words: Moving to a new residence.
Polarity: Neutral.
Literal meaning: Never interpreted literally.

SUN: The Sun is happiness and well-being. This will be a time period when warmth, joy, and good things in general embrace every avenue of your life. The Sun appears to be a ball with either rough, fuzzy edges or rays (lines) going out from it. If it is just a ball with no rays or fuzzy edges, it is not the Sun—it is a ball (see *Ball*). No other symbol, even if coupled with the Sun, can influence the Sun. The Sun outshines everything. The Sun can influence other symbols, but cannot be influenced by them.

Key words: Happiness and well-being.
Polarity: Highly positive.
Literal meaning: Never interpreted literally.

-T-

TABLE: A table means "favor." If the table is by itself, the period of time indicated will be a favorable one for you. You will seem to have the "Midas touch" during this time in that everything you do will turn out favorably for you. No one will be able to "rain on your parade" during this time.

If the table is coupled with any positive symbol, you will collect a favor that is owed you by someone.

If the table is coupled with any negative symbol, it is time for you to repay a favor that you owe someone.

Key word: Favor.
Polarity: Positive.
Literal meaning: Never interpreted literally.

TALL BUILDING: A tall building signifies that you have laid a solid foundation in your personal life as well as your public life.

With dedicated effort you will rise to high achievement in whatever you set your mind to do. Most often this symbol applies to your occupation, but it is not restricted to just that. It relates to any endeavor: your hobby, work in a fraternal organization, charity or volunteer work, crafts, politics, your occupation…whatever.

The key phrase is "with dedicated effort." There are no free rides, but you are guaranteed success "with dedicated effort."

This symbol applies to your entire life and not just the period that it indicates in the tea cup. It is always interpreted by itself; other symbols have no effect on it.

Key words: Solid foundation. Success with dedicated
  effort.

Polarity: Positive.

Literal meaning: Never interpreted literally.

TEAPOT: A teapot indicates that you will develop a deep friendship with someone of your own gender. You will become confidants for each other. In each other you will find a person with whom you can share your deepest thoughts, secrets, and dreams. You will be mutually supportive of each other, and both of your lives will become richer for having known each other.

Most often you will meet this person during the time period indicated. However, occasionally it is someone you already know with whom you will develop a deep friendship during the time period indicated.

Other symbols have no influence on the teapot. The teapot is always interpreted alone.

Key words: Deep friendship with someone of your own
  gender.

Polarity: Positive.

Literal meaning: Never interpreted literally.

TEAR DROP: One tear drop in your tea cup signifies that you will be afflicted with a personal sorrow during the time indicated. If there is more than one tear drop, it will be a great sorrow that will remain in your memory for the rest of your life.

Other symbols have no influence on tear drops.

Key word: Sorrow.
Polarity: Negative.
Literal meaning: Never interpreted literally.

TELEPHONE: The telephone indicates that during the time period you will have an important business engagement. If the telephone is by itself, the engagement will be beneficial to your work or to your status in the community.

If the telephone is coupled with any positive symbol, the engagement will open up new opportunities for you that you hadn't previously anticipated.

If the telephone is coupled with any negative symbol, the engagement will be detrimental to you in some way.

Key words: Important business engagement.
Polarity: Positive.
Literal meaning: Never interpreted literally.

TELESCOPE: A telescope means that you will receive a long-distance telephone call during the report period. This will not be a routine call from someone who usually calls you. It will be from someone whom you either don't know or you have not heard from in years.

If the telephone is by itself, it will be a welcome call that will make you feel good.

If the telephone is coupled with any positive symbol, the call will be highly beneficial to you, bringing you exceptionally good news.

If coupled with any negative symbol, the call will bring you bad news—news that will upset you.

Key words: Long-distance telephone call.
Polarity: Neutral.
Literal meaning: Never interpreted literally.

TELEVISION: If you see a television set in your tea leaves, it means that you will see some event that does not involve you but will have a profound effect on you. The seeing can be done in person or via a television, movie, video cassette, or photograph. This does not apply to mental visions. For example, you might see an auto accident in which an innocent person is hurt or killed by a drunk driver. The experience causes you to become politically active in supporting or creating stiffer laws and penalties for drunk driving.

If the television is coupled with any negative symbol, the experience will be unpleasant.

If coupled with any positive symbol, the experience will be pleasant.

If the television is by itself, the experience will most likely be of an unemotional nature which you will merely observe and learn from.

Key words: You will see an event that will have a profound effect on you.

Polarity: Positive.

Literal meaning: Never interpreted literally.

TENT: A tent means "a temporary situation." During the time period, you will be involved in some situation that will not last.

If the tent is by itself, it will be a situation that you want to have last, but it won't. Perhaps you meet someone with whom you desire a lasting relationship, but it will dissolve as quickly as it started. Perhaps it will be a job that you want to have last, but it won't. The temporary situation will last about two weeks.

If the tent is coupled with any positive symbol, the meaning is the same as if alone except that the temporary situation may last as long as two months.

If the tent is coupled with any negative symbol, the meaning is the same as if alone except that the temporary situation will last less than a week.

Key words: Temporary situation.

Polarity: Slightly negative.

Literal meaning: Never interpreted literally.

THREE SIXES (6 6 6): This is rarely seen, but it is so important that it must be mentioned. If the number 6 appears exactly three times (6 6 6) in a cup, you are in grave danger. The sixes do not have to be side by side; they can be placed anywhere. There must be exactly three—no more, no less—for this interpretation to apply. If there are more or less than three, just interpret them as being the number six as described under the *Numeral* listing.

With three sixes, ignore everything else in the cup. This is the most powerful of evil signs, and you are in the gravest of danger physically, spiritually, and mentally. Most often the danger will be from one person, or perhaps several people, who appear to be friends. Occasionally, the danger will be from a person or persons whom you can readily identify as being a threat. In any case, the warning of the three sixes must be taken very seriously.

You will not come to harm if you successfully identify those who are a danger to you and refuse to go along with any of their ideas, no matter how safe they seem to be. Completely divorce yourself from the threatening people and be cautious and protective at all times. It would be a good idea to confide in someone you trust beyond a shadow of a doubt so they can be supportive and protective of you.

Key words: You are in the gravest of danger.
Polarity: Extremely negative.
Literal meaning: Never interpreted literally.

THRONE: A throne means that you will be placed into a position of authority. This could be a promotion at work, getting elected to some office, or getting a job that has authority as an inherent part of it such as a police officer, guard, etc.

You will handle the authority well if the throne is alone or coupled with any positive symbol.

You will handle authority poorly if the symbol is coupled with any negative symbol.

Key words: Position of authority.

Polarity: Positive.

Literal meaning: Never interpreted literally.

TIGER: A tiger indicates that you will be involved in a situation that you will be unable to handle adequately.

If the tiger is by itself or coupled with any positive symbol, the situation will cause you much work, concern, and emotional drain. You will learn much from it, but you will be unsuccessful in dealing with it.

If the tiger is coupled with any negative symbol, the situation will have some sort of detrimental effect on you. For example, it may cause you to lose your job, or affect your health adversely, and so forth.

Key words: Situation you are unable to handle.

Polarity: Highly negative.

Literal meaning: Never interpreted literally.

TOILET: A toilet signifies health problems. If it is by itself, you will be afflicted with an illness that will last several weeks.

If the toilet is coupled with any positive symbol, your illness will be minor and brief, lasting less than a week.

If the toilet is coupled with any negative symbol, your illness will be serious and will last more than a month. If coupled with a highly negative symbol, it could last a lifetime.

Key words: Health problems.
Polarity: Negative.
Literal meaning: Never interpreted literally.

TORCH: A torch means that you will be called upon to make a sacrifice. If the torch is by itself, the sacrifice is most likely to be financial. If the torch is coupled with any positive symbol, the sacrifice is most likely to be spiritual in the sense that you will do something to help your fellow human.

If the torch is coupled with any negative symbol, your sacrifice is likely to be for a family member or a friend who will not appreciate it.

Key word: Sacrifice.
Polarity: Neutral.
Literal meaning: Never interpreted literally.

TOWEL: Someone is trying to cover up some mistake or misdeed. If the towel is coupled with any negative symbol, the cover-up attempt could be a very serious matter; for example, covering up the skimming of money from the cash register.

If the towel is not coupled with any other symbol, it indicates a relatively minor matter such as covering up a little white lie.

If the towel is coupled with any positive or any neutral polarity symbol, the cover-up is extremely minor and can be ignored.

Key words: Covering up a mistake or misdeed.

Polarity: Negative

Literal meaning: Never interpreted literally.

TRAILER: Any sort of trailer, whether it be one you live in or one you haul things in, signifies that you will depart on an extended trip. Extended means several months at least if the trailer is alone. It can be several years if coupled with any positive symbol.

If coupled with any negative symbol, you won't like the trip. For example, you are drafted and spend several years on duty in a strife-ridden area of the world.

Key words: Extended trip.

Polarity: Neutral.

Literal meaning: If the trailer is coupled with a numeral or an alphabetic letter, interpret the trailer literally.

TRAIN: A train indicates that your life will be a series of related experiences linked together for one common destination. That destination is your goal in life.

Your life will not be a mixture of haphazard experiences related to different goals. Not you. Yours is an organized life headed toward one main goal, and you will not be derailed.

Everything you do will in some way relate to the attainment of that one goal. Like the train, you will press onward, slowly at times, but always steadily, and you will take on cargo (experiences) as you proceed. Those experiences will enable you to reach your destination.

Key words: One goal orientation.

Polarity: Highly positive.

Literal meaning: If the train is coupled with a numeral or an alphabetic letter, interpret the train literally.

TRAY: A tray indicates that you will have an illness that will require you to be bedridden; it also includes injury.

If the tray is by itself, the illness will require you to be bedridden at home, not in a hospital, for at least a week.

If the tray is coupled with any positive symbol, you will be bedridden at home for just a couple days.

If the tray is coupled with any negative symbol, you will be hospitalized.

Key words: Bedridden illness.
Polarity: Negative.
Literal meaning: Never interpreted literally.

TREE: A tree pertains to your family. Family includes your parents, siblings, spouse, and children. It does not include other relatives or in-laws.

By itself, the tree indicates a strong, close-knit family in which there is love, trust, and mutual support.

If the tree is coupled with any positive symbol, your family will have strong healthy genetics and will be predisposed to long, healthy lives.

If the tree is coupled with any negative symbol, your family has no unity or closeness. Yours is a fragmented family whose attitude is "every man for himself."

Key words: Your family.
Polarity: Slightly positive.
Literal meaning: Never interpreted literally.

TRIANGLE: In an otherwise positive cup, this indicates a religious or spiritual experience. In an otherwise negative cup, this means treachery or deceit from someone you trusted and/or loved.

Whether or not the triangle is coupled with other symbols does not matter in the interpretation. What matters is the general polarity of the entire cup.

Key words: Either a spiritual experience or treachery from a friend or loved one. (See above explanation.)
Polarity: Neutral.
Literal meaning: Never interpreted literally.

TRICYCLE: A tricycle means that you need help. You have bitten off more than you can chew in some matter, and you need help if you are to come out of the situation okay.

If the tricycle is by itself, you will receive a little help, but for the most part you are on your own. The help you receive will be sufficient only if you personally exert much time and energy to help yourself.

If the tricycle is coupled with any positive symbol, you will receive plenty of help—not to worry.

If the tricycle is coupled with any negative symbol, you will not receive any help. If it is coupled with a highly negative symbol, you will actually receive opposition that will likely cause you to fail.

Key words: You need help.
Polarity: Negative.
Literal meaning: Never interpreted literally.

TRUCK: Any truck indicates hard work. You will be in a period of plain, old-fashioned hard work. There is no getting out of it, and there will be no help. It will likely mean long hours with little or no relaxation. The period will last from two weeks to a month.

If the truck is by itself, the work will be beneficial. Your efforts will be worth it.

If the truck is coupled with any positive symbol, your work could pay off handsomely for you.

If coupled with any negative symbol, it is a warning that you need to pace yourself and be careful so you don't endanger your health by overwork or injury.

Key words: Period of hard work.

Polarity: Positive.

Literal meaning: If the truck is coupled with a numeral or an alphabetic letter, interpret the truck literally.

TRUNK: A trunk indicates that you lead, or will begin to lead, a nomadic life.

If the trunk is by itself, your nomadic life will last several years. If the trunk is coupled with any positive symbol, your nomadic life will be less than a year.

If the trunk is coupled with a negative symbol, your nomadic ways will likely continue for most of your life.

Key words: Nomadic life.

Polarity: Slightly positive.

Literal meaning: Never interpreted literally.

TURTLE: Don't give up. Just keep pursuing your goal and you will succeed, but it may not occur as quickly as you would like. The turtle indicates that if you just hang tough and have perseverance, you will eventually achieve what you are striving for.

If coupled with a negative symbol, it just indicates that you will encounter some problems or delays, but you will still prevail.

If coupled with a positive symbol, you will have smooth sailing toward your objectives.

Key words: Don't give up. Success is yours if you persevere.
Polarity: Positive.
Literal meaning: Never interpreted literally.

TYPEWRITER: A typewriter pertains to writing occupations such as a writer, editor, reporter, secretary, court reporter, etc. A writer can be a freelance writer, a technical writer, or a person working for a company whose principal duty is to write documents.

The typewriter, whether alone or coupled with other symbols, indicates that your best chance for success is in an occupation associated with writing.

If coupled with a positive symbol, you have excellent potential in the creative writing field.

If coupled with a negative symbol, you have excellent potential in the legal field. For example, court reporter, paralegal, etc.

Key words: Occupation associated with writing.
Polarity: Positive.
Literal meaning: Never interpreted literally.

-*U*-

UFO: An Unidentified Flying Object (UFO) is also called a flying saucer. A UFO in a tea cup is a cardinal symbol of powerful, innate psychic ability.

The only symbols that can be coupled with a UFO are those symbols that indicate some person other than yourself (figure of a person, horse, dog etc.). In these cases, the psychic person is the one indicated by the symbol, and you will receive enlightened guidance from this person.

Also, numerals or alphabetic letters can couple with a UFO. (See the literal meaning below.)

Otherwise the UFO always indicates that you have great psychic ability. The implication is that you should develop it and use it to enrich your life and the lives of others. This is a great gift that should not be ignored.

Key words: Great psychic ability.

Polarity: Highly positive.

Literal meaning: If the UFO is coupled with a numeral or an alphabetic letter, interpret the UFO literally.

UMBRELLA: An umbrella signifies that during the period indicated you will be protected from harm and from situations that are beyond your control.

If the danger occurs because of your own foolish action or poor judgment, the umbrella will not protect you.

The implication is that you will be exposed to a dangerous or detrimental situation during the time period. You have no need to worry as long as you had no part in creating the detrimental situation.

Key words: Protected from dangerous situations beyond your control.

Polarity: Positive.

Literal meaning: Never interpreted literally.

UNDERGARMENTS (PANTIES, BRIEFS, etc.): Undergarments in a tea cup signify that you are overly concerned about sexual matters.

If the undergarment is alone, it means that you think about sexual acts a considerable amount of time. You dwell on sex more than is healthy, and it could lead to promiscuity if it hasn't already.

If the undergarment is coupled with any positive symbol, it means that you frequently relieve your sexual tensions by masturbation.

If the undergarment is coupled with any negative symbol, it means that you engage in sexual experiences to excess. Sex is your only real interest in life. In extreme cases, if the undergarment is coupled with a highly negative symbol such as a coiled snake, you engage in perverse sexual acts.

Key words: Overly concerned about sexual matters.

Polarity: Negative.

Literal meaning: Never interpreted literally.

-*V*-

VALLEY: A valley is the V-shape between two hills or mountains. Thus the valley is automatically coupled to either hills or mountains (see *Hill* and *Mountain*), both of which are positive symbols.

The valley indicates deep personal strength and peace that will assure you success in whatever you do.

If the valley is between two hills, the interpretation is profound spiritual understanding. You will have strength and faith to overcome anything you encounter. No one and nothing can ever defeat you. With this in your cup, you could become a notable leader or teacher. I'm not talking about teaching academic subjects. I'm talking about teaching truth, metaphysics, psychic matters, self-development matters, etc.

If the valley is between two mountains, the interpretation is that you will meet a great challenge with such success that you will gain a certain amount of fame from it.

Be sure you interpret the hills and mountains accurately. Hills are rounded like scoops of ice cream. Mountains are jagged with rather sharp lines and tops.

Key words: Deep personal strength and peace that assures success.

Polarity: Highly positive.

Literal meaning: Never interpreted literally.

VASE: A vase indicates that you have a secret admirer who adores you. If the vase is alone in the cup, your admirer is not likely to ever reveal him or herself to you. The worship is from afar, so to speak, and the admirer is afraid of rejection by you. That is why the admirer will remain secret. If you somehow suspect who it is and make the first move, then the admirer will admit it.

If the vase is coupled with any positive symbol, the admirer will eventually reveal him or herself and you will be pleased. The admirer will not cause you any sort of personal problem.

If the vase is coupled with any negative symbol, the admirer will reveal him or herself and will be a source of personal problems to you.

Key words: Secret admirer.
Polarity: Slightly positive.
Literal meaning: Never interpreted literally.

VINE: A vine indicates that there is information you need to seek in order to benefit yourself in some way. The information will not usually be given to you in time to help you unless you deliberately search it out.

If the vine is coupled to another symbol, it will indicate the nature of the information you must seek. For example, if coupled with a dollar sign ($), it indicates the time is right for you to obtain some money, but you must seek out the way to do it. If coupled with a bat it indicates there is unseen treachery awaiting you, and you must seek out the treachery in order to neutralize it and thus avoid it.

If the vine is not coupled to another symbol, it simply means that you need to seek out more information concerning whatever you are doing in order to be more successful. The influence of the vine is only for a week or two around the period indicated.

Key words: Hidden information you must seek out.
Polarity: Positive.
Literal meaning: Never interpreted literally.

VISE: A vise signifies that you will find yourself in a very difficult situation that will squeeze you very hard. The squeeze may be financial, physical, spiritual, or in a number of other ways.

If the vise is alone, the situation will be serious enough to cause you a great deal of distress.

If the vise is coupled with any positive symbol, the situation will be one that is thrust on you without you contributing to the problem. Because of this, you will successfully overcome the problem with a minimal amount of distress or loss.

If the vise is coupled with any negative symbol, you will be responsible for the problem because of your words or actions. As a result, the squeeze on you will be great and you will not overcome the problem completely. You will carry the scars from this encounter for the rest of your life.

Key words: A very difficult situation.
Polarity: Highly negative.
Literal meaning: Never interpreted literally.

-*W*-

WAGON: A wagon means work. You will be working hard during the indicated time period.

If the wagon is alone, you will have a temporary increase in workload that should last about one week to six weeks.

If the wagon is coupled with any positive symbol, you will find employment if you are currently unemployed. If you are currently employed, you will be given increased responsibility that will most likely accompany a promotion and salary increase.

If coupled with any negative symbol, you will have a great deal of hard work thrust on you, without any extra pay for it, and with no appreciation shown.

Key word: Work.
Polarity: Positive.
Literal meaning: Never interpreted literally.

WALL: A wall means that during the time period indicated you will develop a major misunderstanding between yourself and some other person which will bring you both much unhappiness and bitterness.

The wall by itself indicates that the misunderstanding is significant and will destroy your relationship with the other person unless you take the initiative to resolve the problem promptly. You will have to resolve the problem within a week, otherwise it will be too late to hope for reconciliation.

If the wall is coupled with any positive symbol, there is hope for reconciliation up to two months, and the other person will welcome the chance, but it is up to you to make the first move.

If the wall is coupled with any negative symbol, there is little hope for reconciliation. The hurt will have been too deep on both sides.

Key word: Misunderstanding.
Polarity: Negative.
Literal meaning: Never interpreted literally.

WATER: Water is difficult to see in a cup. It might appear as a placid pool, or it might look like large waves in a surf. It is easy to overlook water. Examine the cup carefully from all angles because placid pools are fairly common. Water is the giver of life, hence it is interpreted to mean good health. Water is not affected one way or the other by the polarity of nearby symbols.

At a minimum, water in your tea cup assures you of good health during the time period indicated and at least several months on each side of the time period. More typically, it indicates good health for the entire year.

If water appears several times in the same cup, then the good health will be for life.

Key words: Good health.

Polarity: Positive.

Literal meaning: If water is coupled with a numeral or an alphabetic letter, interpret the water literally.

WEDGE SHAPE: If you have a wedge shape in your tea cup, someone is trying to come between you and someone or something you want.

If the wedge shape is not coupled with anything, then someone is trying to come between you and some other person. For example, trying to break up your romance with someone, or trying to alienate you from your boss, and so forth.

If the wedge shape is coupled with some other symbol, blend the meanings of the two in order to determine just what is going on. For example, if the wedge shape is coupled with a desk, someone is trying to either get your job or is trying to get you fired or transferred.

Key words: Someone is trying to come between you and someone or something you want.
Polarity: Negative.
Literal meaning: Never interpreted literally.

WHALE: A whale indicates that you will be greatly concerned about what appears to be a huge problem or potential problem, and the problem will turn out to be either nonexistent or of very minor importance. You will worry much about nothing.

If the whale is coupled with any negative symbol, you will worry to the point of being ill. An example of the kind of worry I am referring to is this: There is a rumor where you work that there is going to be a massive layoff due to an economic downturn. All employees with less than four years tenure will be let go before the end of the month. You have only two years with the company, and you really need your job because of high mortgage payments, a new baby is about to arrive, etc., so you worry yourself sick about it. As it turns out, the rumor was groundless. There was no layoff at all. Your job was secure all the time.

Key words: Great worry about nothing.
Polarity: Slightly negative.
Literal meaning: Never interpreted literally.

WHEEL: The wheel signifies that you are generally an indecisive person. As a result, your life seems to flow with circumstances rather than by your own actions. The implication is that you must learn to be decisive if you want to achieve anything in your life and realize any sense of fulfillment.

If the wheel is coupled with any positive symbol, someone will enter your life who will help you to overcome your indecisiveness.

If the wheel is by itself, the implication is that you have the ability to overcome your indecisiveness by yourself if you really want to and you are willing to work at it.

If coupled with any negative symbol, the implication is that you will live your entire life with very little accomplishment due primarily to your indecisiveness.

Key word: Indecisiveness.

Polarity: Negative.

Literal meaning: If coupled with a numeral or an alphabetic letter, interpret the wheel literally.

WHEELBARROW: The wheelbarrow indicates that you will succeed in achieving your goals only by hard, steady work. Success won't come easy for you, but you are guaranteed success through hard, steady work Don't expect much help from others. It will be pretty much a one-person effort—yours.

Key words: Success through hard, steady work.
Polarity: Positive.
Literal meaning: Never interpreted literally.

WIG: Any sort of wig in your tea cup indicates that you will be involved with the law during the time period indicated. The involvement could be anything from jury duty, to getting a traffic ticket, to becoming a law officer, to being arrested or sued, and so on.

If the wig is by itself in the cup, your involvement will be either as a participant (jury duty, for example) or for some minor infraction such as a traffic ticket. It could even be your participation in some program such as taking a citizen's ride around with a patrol officer.

If the wig is coupled with any positive symbol, your involvement is more likely to be something more important like you becoming a law officer, testifying in a court of law, or giving a deposition.

If the wig is coupled with any negative symbol, you will be in some sort of legal trouble, perhaps being sued, being arrested, or put into jail.

Key words: Involved with the law.
Polarity: Neutral.
Literal meaning: Never interpreted literally.

WINDOW: The window means that you have great innate psychic ability. If the window is alone, you are already aware of your psychic ability even though you may not necessarily have done much with it. All your life you have seemed to know things. You sense things before they happen. You seem to be able to read people easily and see right through their games and masquerades.

If the window is coupled with any positive symbol, your psychic ability is very close to the surface and you can develop it quite easily if you wish to.

If coupled with any negative symbol, it will take a great deal of persistence, self-discipline, and dedicated effort for you to develop your psychic ability because you have created mental blocks which must be overcome.

Key words: Innate psychic ability.
Polarity: Positive.
Literal meaning: Never interpreted literally.

WISHBONE: A wishbone, if not broken, indicates that a wish or desire will be fulfilled and become reality during the time period indicated in the tea cup.

If the wishbone is broken so that a piece of it is missing, your wish will not be fulfilled.

If the wishbone is cracked or broken but all the pieces are present, your wish will be fulfilled at some later time beyond the time scope of the tea cup.

Key words: Unbroken—wish granted. A piece missing— wish not granted. Broken with all pieces present— wish granted at some later time.

Polarity: Positive.
Literal meaning: Never interpreted literally.

WOLF (FACE): A wolf face means that someone is being deceitful to you. This is usually a person whom you think you know fairly well and have trust in. This person pretends to be on your side, to be supportive of you, to be your ally. In truth, this person is working behind your back to bring about your downfall. Most of the time this deceit pertains to your place of work, but it can apply to other avenues of your life as well.

If the wolf face is by itself, you won't find out about the deceit until it is nearly too late to prevent damage to yourself. However, "nearly" implies that you have a chance of rectifying the situation at the last moment.

If the wolf face is coupled with any positive symbol, you will become suspicious in plenty of time to expose the deceitful person and rectify the situation.

If the wolf face is coupled with any negative symbol, the damage to you will be done before you are aware of what happened.

Key words: Deceit against you.
Polarity: Negative.
Literal meaning: Never interpreted literally.

WORM: A worm means humility and patience. If the worm is by itself, it means you need to learn humility and patience.

If the worm is coupled with any positive symbol, you already are a humble and patient person.

If the worm is coupled with any negative symbol, you have lost all of your humility and patience, causing you to become a person whom others do not care to be around very much.

Key words: Humility. Patience.
Polarity: Positive.
Literal meaning: Never interpreted literally.

WREATH: A wreath is the symbol of sorrow, usually due to a death. The wreath sometimes signifies sorrow over something other than a death if it is coupled with a symbol that indicates it.

If the wreath is by itself, you will mourn the death of someone who is important to you. It could be a person or a pet.

The polarity of nearby symbols does not affect the wreath, but the meanings of the symbols do affect the wreath. For example, if the wreath is coupled with any symbol that indicates money, you will mourn the loss of a great deal of your money or property. If coupled with a house, you will lose your home, and so on.

Key words: Sorrow over a loss, usually a death.
Polarity: Negative.
Literal meaning: Never interpreted literally.

Appendix

Crystals and Tea Leaf Reading

What is an appendix on crystals doing in a book on tea leaf reading?

Simple. I use quartz crystals to aid me in my tea leaf reading.

At first I was just going to write a couple brief paragraphs about my use of crystals and let it go at that. Then I decided to write a more in-depth description of my crystals and how I use them.

You do not need to use crystals of any kind in order to accurately read tea leaves. This appendix is just an added attraction, so to speak, in case you wish to expand your horizons.

Quartz Crystals

Quartz crystals are a natural formation that have the ability to store energy, store intelligence, and to focus and intensify energy and intelligence.

Quartz crystals grow in clusters. Most commonly each crystal, in its natural state, resembles a miniature pointed shaft similar to Washington's Monument. One end is rooted in the cluster and the other end is a six-faceted point. When a crystal is broken or cut from the cluster, the rooted end is blunt.

Occasionally a crystal grows in such a manner that both ends contain six-faceted points. This effectively doubles the power of the crystal.

All crystals, regardless of size or shape, store and focus energy and intelligence. This is why they can be so valuable as an aid in reading tea leaves or in doing any sort of psychic work.

How I Use My Crystals

I have many crystals that I have collected over the years. One is a fairly rare one that I carry in my pocket. The others are in a display in one of my bookcases; these I use for meditation from time to time.

My pocket crystal: My pocket crystal is fairly rare. It is two and one-quarter inches long and both ends are six-faceted points. In addition, three "baby" crystals are on the side of the large crystal. Each of these "babies" has six-faceted points at both ends also.

The crystal is clear and unblemished. It is a powerful tool for me, and I carry it with me at all times in a small black jewelry pouch. (The color of the pouch has no significance; it just happens to be one of several I have.) The pouch protects the crystal from being scratched by keys or coins in my pocket.

My crystal necklace: This crystal is a common one having one six-faceted point. It is one and a quarter inches long, and the blunt end has an eyelet so I thread a small silver chain through it and wear it as a necklace.

Note: I also suspend it on the silver chain and use it as a pendulum for psychic work, but this has nothing to do with using it for tea leaf reading.

This crystal is fairly clear and has a few minor blemishes, but it is still quite satisfactory. I wear it around my neck occasionally.

My aventurine crystal: This is a smooth, polished, heart-shaped crystal that is two inches across. It is a dark green stone with a metallic iridescence and is associated with good luck, some healing, and it affects the pituitary gland.

Crystals and Reading Tea Leaves

The crystal stores and focuses energy. The six-faceted end of a crystal contains "sending" planes and "receiving" planes. This means that the crystal enhances your natural ability to send energy and also to receive energy.

The crystal must be within the field of your aura in order for you to use it. On average, your aura extends two to three feet in every direction from your body. I always have the crystal on my person—either wearing it, holding it, or in my pocket.

When I read tea leaves, the crystal focuses the energy of the tea leaf patterns, enhancing my perceptive powers so that I see the symbols clearly and accurately. The crystal also sharpens my understanding so I gain more complete knowledge of exactly what the tea leaf messages are.

Simplistically, the quartz crystal seems to do for energies what a magnifying glass does for objects—it magnifies them.

I have read tea leaves accurately for many years without having a crystal to help me. Likewise, you have read printed words for many years without using a magnifying glass. When you want to see the fine print—to see the smallest detail—you reach for the magnifying glass.

When I want to sense the faintest energy—to understand the greatest detail—I reach for my quartz crystal.

That is how you can use a quartz crystal in reading tea leaves or in enhancing any psychic ability. You enhance both your receiving ability and your sending ability.

In my psychic work, I use crystals to enhance my ability to send love, healing, messages, etc. to others. So can you.

My aventurine crystal was given to me in 1988 by my friend and fellow author, Phyllis Galde, who is an expert on crystals. She told me this particular crystal was a great aid for creative visualization and all creative endeavors in general. I have found it to be an effective tool not only for my creative writing but also to enhance my perception and analysis for tea leaf reading.

Care of Crystals

Crystals store energy—any energy whether it be positive or negative, beneficial or detrimental. You want your crystals to be charged with your energies, not with the negative energies from someone else.

What you need to do is discharge the crystals from time to time and recharge them with your energy. It is a simple matter to do both of these things.

Discharging crystals: Periodically bury the crystal in a box or bag of *non-iodized* sea salt overnight. The sea salt absorbs the energy from the quartz crystal and diffuses that energy. This neutralizes the crystal. You can neutralize several crystals at the same time.

The sea salt is quite inexpensive and is available from health food stores and even from some supermarkets. A box of this salt will last a lifetime if it doesn't get wet. Common table salt and iodized sea salt should not be used because both have been altered chemically by a manmade process that negates the ability of the salt crystals to absorb the energies from the crystal.

I generally neutralize both of my crystals overnight about every two weeks. I do it more often if they are exposed to a strong negative atmosphere. For example, if I have my crystal and I am in the presence of a strongly negative person for more than a couple minutes, I will neutralize the crystal that very same night.

Charging the quartz crystal: Hold the crystal in one hand for five minutes. Then hold it in the other hand for another five minutes. This ten-minute charge will last about two weeks if you don't keep the crystal on your person. Of course, if you carry or wear the crystal, the charge will be maintained without having to be recharged. For example, suppose you charge the quartz crystal with your hands and then put the crystal in a drawer for a week. After a week you decide to carry or wear it for a day. That one day's wear will recharge the crystal for another two weeks. If you go two weeks without having the crystal within your aura, you will have to recharge it with your hands.

If you have two crystals, you can charge them both at the same time. Hold one in each hand for five minutes. Then switch the crystals to the other hand and hold them for another five minutes.

I make it a practice of meditating on positive, constructive thoughts during the ten minutes I am charging my crystals. I believe this to be greatly beneficial, and I recommend you do the same. However, you don't have to do this type of meditation in order to charge a crystal.

Index